CROSSING THE SACRED LINE

Women's Search for Political Power

CROSSING THE SACRED LINE

Women's Search for Political Power

Abhilasha Kumari
Sabina Kidwai

Orient Longman

The research for this book was done under the aegis of the Friedrich-Ebert-Stiftung.

CROSSING THE SACRED LINE

ORIENT LONGMAN LIMITED

Registered Office
3-6-272 Himayatnagar, Hyderabad 500 029 (A.P.), INDIA

Other Offices
Bangalore, Bhopal, Bhubaneshwar, Calcutta, Chandigarh, Chennai, Ernakulam, Guwahati, Hyderabad, Jaipur, Lucknow, Mumbai, New Delhi, Patna

First published 1998
Reprinted 1999

ISBN 81 250 1434 9

Printed in India at
Baba Barkha Nath Printers
New Delhi 110 015

Published by
Orient Longman Limited
1/24 Asaf Ali Road
New Delhi 110 002

Foreword

As early as in 1917, Indian women raised the issue of representation in politics, which at that time meant a demand for universal adult franchise. Emphasizing the right to vote as basic to a citizen's participation in the public domain, Sarojini Naidu addressed the Secretary of State, Montague, in 1917 by saying: "When such a franchise is being drawn upon, women may be recognized as people and it may be worded in such terms as will not disqualify for sex, but allow our women the same opportunities of representation as our men."[1] In 1996 the claim for equal opportunities with respect to representation of Indian women in the legislature is as pertinent as it was eighty years ago. Even though the Indian Constitution of 1948 guarantees equal social, economic and political right to women, the representation of women in political bodies is still abysmally low. This is sharply contrasted by the fact that the participation of Indian women in elections has steadily increased since the first general elections held in 1952. In the period from 1952 to 1980 women's participation in the elections increased by 12 per cent whereas the turnout of men increased by merely 6 per cent. In 1996, the turnout for women was 47.75 per cent whereas for men it was 52.25 per cent.

The increase in the turnout of women in elections has, however, not been translated into a larger number of women being represented in the legislative bodies. The percentage of women in the national parliament after the general elections in May 1996 still amounts to only 6.7 per cent of the total seats, and even in earlier parliaments never exceeded 8.1 per cent. It is evident that in the world's largest democracy, politics are

1 Natesan, G.A. (ed.), *Speeches and Writings of Sarojini Naidu*, 1918.

clearly dominated by men. Women do not share the power of decision-making and are subsequently not involved in policy-making in the Indian democracy. Against this backdrop, 33 per cent reservation of seats in the legislature (viz. the national parliament and State Assemblies) as proposed in September 1996 through the 81st Amendment to the Indian Constitution is now supported even by those citizens who for a long time were optimistic that the political system would open up for women and prove that reservation for women is futile. Today, it seems that reservation for women is the only recourse for equal representation and decision-making. At the same time there is a recognition of the need to go beyond the reservation policy.

The increasing relevance of women as voters in the democratic system is not adequately reflected in the constitution of institutions through which political power is acquired, that is, the political parties. The ratio of women in political parties across the country and across ideologies ranges from 5-12 per cent of the membership. Although political parties in the seventies began to realize the importance of the female vote bank and did set up women's wings, little progress has been made. Women have neither participated in parties in significantly high numbers nor have they acquired higher positions of decision-making. So called 'women's issues' have not been taken up by parties in a serious manner nor translated into programmes, policies and legislation.

Crossing the Sacred Line: Women's Search for Political Power attempts to look at the underlying reasons for the marginalisation of women and 'women's issues' in political parties. By looking into the histories, ideologies, and political manifestos as well as at the organisational structures of three national and two regional parties, the authors have tried to gain better insights into the position of women in the political system. In-depth interviews with women politicians highlight the first -hand experiences and perspectives of select women who have successfully climbed their way up to positions of power. The book is born out of a burning concern with the question of political participation of women. It is hoped that it will contribute to overcoming the existing mechanisms of discrimination against women in the political system.

The Friedrich-Ebert-Stiftung (FES) is a non-profit, public interest institution committed to the concept and basic values of social democracy in its educational and policy-oriented work. Aiming at the strengthening of democratic structures, FES promotes training and policy-oriented research programmes in Germany and—in cooperation with partner organisations—in more than 80 countries across the world. In South Asia, it has set up offices in Colombo, Delhi, Islamabad and Kathmandu. In India, the Friedrich-Ebert-Stiftung has been working in the area of industrial relations, labour and social policy, social security, self-help initiatives/micro-enterprises, women's economic and political empowerment, regional cooperation, media and environment.

In order to facilitate the discussion on crucial issues related to the development process in India, the Friedrich-Ebert-Stiftung publishes a number of contributions of which this publication is a part. The views expressed in this publication do not necessarily reflect those of the Friedrich-Ebert-Stiftung.

Luise Rürup

Friedrich-Ebert-Stiftung
New Delhi

December 1996

Contents

Introduction

Fifty years of independence has made many Indians look back to assess what we have and have not achieved in the past five decades. It is in this context that it becomes imperative to see what fifty years of independence has given to Indian women. As a citizen of this country how much space has the political system given the Indian women to play an active role in the political processes. The statute books may well be replete with provisions regarding political rights (perhaps gained with less effort than her counterparts in other countries), but the question that must be answered is: Despite constituting nearly 50 per cent of the population, she remains marginal to the democratic process, in her own thinking and in the minds of others. We have recognised the marginalisation of certain classes and castes, and the need to redress these imbalances, although after considerable struggle. However, the marginalisation of women from the political process has yet to be recognised and looked at with equal seriousness.

What does access to power mean in a democracy and the way it works in a country like India? Our political system works through political parties who contend for power by invoking popular support. Therefore, it is evident that if women want to share power they have to make a place for themselves within the political parties through which our democratic system operates. The experience of the last fifty years shows their inability to find or create "this space". Recent studies indicate that there has been no significant change in either the nature of women's functioning or in the parties' approach to women and women's issues. How far is the concern for gender equality reflected in the day-to-day functioning of political parties? If we look at the issue of women's participation (till the 1993 elections), it is immediately apparent that political parties have generally given less importance to women's issues in terms of ideology, either as priority in their electoral manifesto or in terms of the number and importance of the position that women occupied in individual political parties. This apathy is reflected very clearly if we look at the number of women in our Parliament.

TABLE I

Participation of Women in Lok Sabha Elections

Election year	Voting Percentage of Men	Voting Percentage of Women	Seats contested by Women	Seats won by Women	Total Seats	Percentage of Women Members
1952	53.00	37.10	51	22	499	4.40
1957	56.00	39.60	70	27	500	5.40
1962	62.10	46.60	68	34	503	6.70
1967	66.70	55.50	66	31	523	5.90
1971	69.70	49.15	86	22	521	4.20
1977	65.62	54.91	70	19	544	3.40
1980	57.69	51.29	142	28	544	5.14
1984	63.61	68.17	159	44	544	8.10
1989	70.90	43.90	189	27	517	5.30
1991	52.56	47.43	325	39	544	7.16
1996	—	—	491	39	543	7.18

Source: *Why Women in Legislatures* by Susheela Kaushik, November 1996

Women are not even seen as a vote bank to be approached and canvassed, as it is expected that once the men are mobilised, women will merely endorse their choice of party and candidate. Male candidates rarely have access to the female electorate and there are not enough women involved in campaigns to be able to reach out to a sizable section of women even in the cities and larger towns. As a result, the exposure of women to political debates and issues has always remained indirect, and almost exclusively on the basis of what is reported to them by the males in the family. Women are not made to feel that they need to be actively involved in a process that requires them to be guided by rational self-interest. Moreover, the perception that politics is a world of men, for which women have neither the predilection nor the requisite knowledge, has been actively encouraged.

The exposure of women to political debates and issues has always remained indirect, and almost exclusively on the basis of what is reported to them by the males in the family.

Unquestioning Acceptance of Traditional Notions

It is the contention of this study that many of the "myths" about women's role in politics have been accepted and passed on unquestioningly, because none of the political parties questioned traditional notions of women's role or status in society. Political participation has been primarily associated with political activity in the public realm, whereas women have been primarily perceived as belonging to the private or the domestic realm. This has influenced women's attitudes to politics and political participation and created a hesitancy among women to involve themselves with "what was perceived as politics". The conclusions drawn have been that women are just not interested in politics, primarily because of "their own backwardness". It is odd that when we talk of other marginalised groups in relation to whether or not they should have access to power, the question of access to that right is not discussed as being contingent upon the capabilities, education, or awareness of the group concerned. These rights are assumed to accrue to those groups on principles and values related to our belief in a democratic system of governance "of the people and by the people", but such issues become important when the question of women's participation is raised. Not all working class and caste groupings are endowed with democratic consciousness, but the necessity of including them in the political process is never denied. Why, then, is the question of women's marginalisation looked at so differently?

In order to understand the negligible role that women play in the democratic process, it is imperative to look at the problem both in its historical context and in the current scenario. Is the problem located in our historical past, in our religious and social traditions, or in the ideologies of political parties, or even in the democratic system as a whole as it functions in our country? We felt that one source of marginalisation might have been the political parties. If that is so, how did this situation come about? Were all parties the same and can they all be conveniently clubbed under the blanket of patriarchy and condemned or were there differences and if so what were these? To answer these questions it becomes imperative to take a closer look at political parties to understand the cause of women's marginalisation—organisationally, ideologically and historically —in the kind of ways in which they have responded to specific political issues relating to women e.g. Muslim Women's Bill or *sati* to name a few.

New Ways of Looking at the Issue

Women's participation in politics is without doubt an important step towards social equality, economic development and national and international peace. But opinions differ regarding the nature of participation and the indicators used to measure it. Due to the lack of a gender-sensitive non-discriminatory approach, the relevance of this issue is often obfuscated by the absence of formal barriers to women's participation, and this tends to make us overlook certain social realities. If rights are not utilised, and if the process of development continues to adversely affect women, then, as Kasturi and Mazumdar point out, "it is necessary to look for hidden barriers to women's political participation."[1]

In India, as elsewhere, an important thrust of feminist social science has been to make women visible, and audible in history and society, and to highlight their contribution to society.

In India, as elsewhere, an important thrust of feminist social science has been to make women visible, and audible in history and society, and to highlight their contribution to society. This endeavour is at least partially in response to what is characterised as a historical patriarchal conspiracy designed to exclude women's contribution to civilisation and society from due recognition. Just as society's legitimacy myths, written historical records and the production of authoritative self-knowledge, have all been controlled by the male, politics has traditionally been viewed as a male domain. Not many analysts have undertaken intensive studies bearing upon women's role in politics, specially of women from the lower classes, and fewer still have looked deep into the issues related to women's participatory potential and the empirical reality. As a result, not much informative analysis is available about women in politics especially from earlier periods. This does not prove the fundamental inability of women to be political; rather, it only catalogues the kind of prejudice and deprivation with which women are confronted. In this context, this study aims to construct "authoritative self-knowledge" through women's own experience in politics.

Looking Beyond Numbers: The first step in looking at the entire question with a new perspective would be to move away

[1] Kasturi, Leela and Mazumdar, Vina, *Political Participation of Women in Developing Countries*, Centre for Women's Development Studies (Unpublished).

from the empiricist tradition of research that uses head-counts as a measure for the level and quality of women's participation in the political process. The logic that takes the total number of female voters in any general election as the relevant measure, would present a rosy picture, but it would be totally disproportionate to reality. For, despite the fact that a large number of women vote, they cannot be argued to have a significant influence on the political strategy and agenda of the politics of the country. Similarly, the number of women in political parties cannot be an accurate, and certainly not the only, measure of the rolc and status allotted to them within a particular party, in terms of their role and power in determining its ideological positions as well as in its organisational structure. Nor can the current trend of evaluating women's political participation in terms of their visibility in government be correct, since this limits our perceptions to the visible minority. Moreover, even the most outstanding women leaders have not always been concerned, or in touch, with women's problems and needs, and have generally tended not to promote women's issues in either government or in party fora.

The indicators used to measure women's political participation must be defined in terms of structure, not numbers. Have women been assimilated into the basic structure of the parties that work within our democracy? Are they perceived as potential activists and candidates at all levels of the organisation? Do they have access to power and training at all levels of the party hierarchy? Has the presence of an increasing number of women in the political arena resulted in the parties recognising a women's agenda within the wider agenda? What is the role of women in the day-to-day functioning of these parties and how far do the political formulations of these parties hinder or accelerate women's active participation? What is the nature of the relationship between men and women within the party in relation to power-sharing? These indicators are by no means exhaustive.

Even if we were to look at the issue purely in terms of numbers—and at times numbers *are* important, especially in a democratic set-up which functions through numerically influential pressure groups—the picture is equally grim. The number of women involved in politics is quite dismal, both in terms of real numbers and as a proportion of the number of men similarly involved. The questions that need to be asked in this connection are: Is it merely the fact that not enough women come into politics, or is it that women are simply not mobilised, nor ideologically and physically trained to participate in politics the way men are? How do political parties look at the question of participation—do they make a conscious effort to mobilise different sections of society, especially women and, if so, with what strategy? Do political parties perceive women as an important segment of the political context, both as participants and as a potential vote bank?

Influence of Social Hierarchy: Another important methodological weakness in the way women's political participation has been studied is the treatment of women as a uniform, homogenous group rather than as differentiated by caste, class, religion and political agenda. Moreover, even within this homogenous group, attention has been focused on a small number of upper-class women who have played important roles in the national movement, etc., excluding reference to the role that women have played in peasants' and workers' struggles. It is important to recognise that different classes are marked by variegated interests and that these are reflected in the difference in demands. Women have to be recognised as a category within each class, with many common, and many different, problems and objectives. We have tried to focus on women's perception of their own identity or identities and how they negotiate and prioritise them in a political context.

At another level, to phrase the questions and expected answers in terms of a man-woman conflict, misses the point and also trivialises the issue. The study endeavours to move beyond such simplistic understanding to more complex structural and ideological aspects of women's marginalisation in politics and specially within political parties.

The Emerging Context

As mentioned earlier, in the more standard analyses of women's political participation, the indicators of the utilisation of political rights have been assumed to be *voting behaviour, candidacy, and holding of public offices.* These indicators, though not the only ones relevant to the inquiry, express some important changes in the nature of women's political participation in recent years.

Women as Voters: Generally in India, registration and participation of women as voters is less than that of men (see Table 1). In the recent past, records show that there has been an increase in the percentage of women who vote. Such participation is also contingent on the mobilisation efforts made by political parties, and the general awareness among the community of the importance of women exercising their franchise. Again, a note of caution is required, lest it be assumed that political participation always indicates political awareness on the part of the woman voter.[2] Usually, however, countries that do hold regular elections show an improved recognition of women as a political constituency and parties and candidates tend to adopt pro-women stances and appeal specifically to women's votes, especially at the time of elections. This becomes very evident when we look at consecutive elections in the Indian context, wherein there is a growing consciousness of the need to woo the woman voter and the need to pay lip-service to the needs of women, if nothing else, in the election manifestos.

Status within Parties: It has often been claimed that

2 Kumari, Abhilasha, and Kidwai, Sabina, *Illusion of Power*, Friedrich Ebert Stiftung, New Delhi, 1994.

women's position in political parties is affected by the nature of the political system. In fact, irrespective of whether it is a single-party system, a two-party system or a multiple-party system, the position of women within these structures has not been qualitatively different, the difference being more of degree than of kind.

Parties that led the national movements against colonial powers were compelled to mobilise women's support. As a result, many of them formed women's organisations within the parties as part of their overall effort to combat colonialism. However, once in power, these women's wings were more or less marginalised and assigned areas that primarily dealt with women and children. Women's organisations thus ended up playing a supportive role to the male leadership in power, and the leaders of such organisations were seldom women with independent political careers.

Moreover, it appears to be a convention, if not a rule (which persists even today), that the women who joined these organisations were women from leading political families. The few women who were an exception to this norm were chosen for, and they themselves preferred, more important positions than being part of the women's wing of the party. The morality of such women who had no kin connections is usually questioned and their name is usually associated with influential male politicians, in keeping with the traditional assumption that a woman is fundamentally incapable of achieving success on her own.

It must also be recognised that very few of the women's organisations of political parties are marked by any kind of feminist perspective. The women's movement in developing countries has tended to place greater emphasis on issues of survival and development that affect all members of society, rather than only those affecting women. They have gone to great lengths to avoid charges of separatism in the hope that women's issues would be recognised as important general issues of

> The women's movement in developing countries has tended to place greater emphasis on issues of survival and development that affect all members of society, rather than only those affecting women.

development, thereby rejecting the separatist approach of some Western feminists. Disillusionment and confrontation with men came only when they persistently ignored women's needs or took hostile action that affected their interests.

Neither during the freedom struggle nor in independent India were the women's wings of major political parties characterised by radicalism. Such criticism has resulted in some women leaders now taking a greater interest in women's issues than they did earlier. Admitting their error in not articulating women's issues adequately within the party hierarchy, these politicians have started to look for effective ways to influence parties. Simultaneously, party leaderships have increasingly come to recognise the under-representation of women at all levels within their parties. Even then some, among women politicians, still persist with the understanding that the endeavour of leaders should be the overall welfare the people rather than of merely a section of them.

As of now, all the political parties have women's wings controlled by women. They work as a pressure group in the party, and usually consist of two groups. The first consists of women who aspire to participate in the higher political hierarchy and join the women's cells within their parties as a first step for entry into the political realm. The other category of women are those already successfully established in the political hierarchy and assigned executive status in these cells to give credibility to the women's wing, to make the base of the party amongst women sound and lasting. At present, national and regional parties are unanimous about projecting a liberal and progressive image for the obvious reason of impressing a vital social segment. However, women's organisations have been given very little power and have virtually no say in decision-making and important policy matters. Male leaders do not hesitate in segregating women, and issues related to them, from general policy matters and in taking isolated policy stances. There are no organised attempts or programmes to train potential women leaders as future leaders. And even though these organisations have brought women together and provided a common platform to strive for the betterment of fellow women as well as an opportunity for training for political status, they have also become breeding grounds of rivalry and jealous competition amongst women aspiring for power. The fact that male politicians continue to exercise control over both their opportunity and access to political power has driven factional wedges down the rank and file of these organisations.

Local Government and Legislation: The number of women in politics at the local level has been very small, and their influence negligible. Prior to 1990, the women in local politics were generally either politicians who had lost membership of higher institutions, or those who were given such an opportunity to serve the purpose of publicity. In many cases, the motive was partially also to satisfy the aspirations of these few women, since they could then be kept under virtual political control and denied higher aspirations.

After 1993, women's participation in local governments increased quite radically, with the enactment of the legislation providing 33 per cent reservation of seats for women in local bodies. The Panchayati Raj legislation and its effective implementation has added another level in political participation. This is of great significance, since this grassroot level participation will considerably broaden the base of women's participation in politics. According to a report by ILO's Rural Employment Branch, although women have been active in peasant organisations, their role has stopped short of positions of leadership. Their role in the trade union movement has also been marginal, and as a result, many problems specific to women's work have not been addressed. Local governments, workers' organisations, trade unions, etc., are all training grounds for participation in higher levels of government. The insignificant presence of women at these levels is an important indicator of two basic facts: one, that women who are planted at the top often lack the kind of training required for effective participation; two, society is unable to accept women in politics, especially at the grassroot level. On the other hand, there are middle-class women who are assigned to these frontal organisations of the party and it is their experience which is represented at the higher levels of the party. Whatever the basis for this, the lacuna does exist, it can be felt even within more ideologically progressive parties. It is important to realise, in this context, that today's mobilisation is a response to the necessity created by reservations and the pressure of women voting as groups on such issues as prohibition, rather than recognition of the importance of women's political participation.

Women in Office: Despite women's right to public office, there exists a tremendous disparity between the number of men and women holding public office. It has been the pattern to give women Ministers portfolios in the social service sector—Health, Education, Social Welfare, etc.—portfolios in which women's nurturing qualities are expected to find full expression. Even within the political arena, responsibilities thus have been consciously or unconsciously divided into women's and men's areas, with what are perceived to be the relatively 'soft posts' usually coming to women and the 'hard ones' going to men—each according to 'their nature', as it were.

New Pressure Groups: The period after the conclusion of the Women's Decade has witnessed the emergence of some new groups that have displayed a more focused, realistic and radical strategy for tackling women's social and economic problems, not hesitating to confront authority in support of their demands. We have also seen a reorientation of some of the old organisations and the emergence of new ones (NGOs). Political parties have begun to recognise women as a potential source of support and are, therefore, ready to adopt a somewhat pro-woman stand and offer greater support to women's organisations.

At the same time, there has been a resistance to women's demand for equality in political circles, at both the national and the lower levels of government. One hopes that reservations for women at these levels will prove to be at least a partial remedy. The rise of religious fundamentalism has also had a negative impact in terms of defining a conservative role for women in society and restricting their participation on an equal basis.

Methodology

The questions and concerns raised earlier, encouraged us to look for the hidden barriers within political parties. For this purpose we chose the three major political parties representing the three wings of Indian politics—the right (the BJP), the centre (the Congress (I)), and the left (the CPI(M))—to study in detail their functioning at all levels of organisation. The objective of this study is to examine how various political parties view women ideologically and, in the world of practical politics, what they expect of their women's wing, and the nature of the relationship of the women's wing with the rest of the party, in both historical and synchronic terms. We have specifically sought to evaluate their performance in relation to issues relating to women and women's rights, the involvement of women's wings in these and other national/international issues. The study also examines whether the emergence of regional parties like the Samajwadi Party in Uttar Pradesh has resulted in any significant expansion of the space traditionally allotted to women for the exercise of theii political will.

Although considerable work has already been done in the area of women and political participation, specially on the success stories, the role of women political activists within the party hierarchy has been little investigated. We have attempted to redress this imbalance, with special focus on the reasons for these differences between the comparatively successful women politicians and the grassroot level women party workers. We have tried to reconstruct the evolution of parties through their responses to certain issues. No attempt is made at setting down any chronology of events, the focus is primarily on issues. Most importantly, this study has attempted to reconstruct, from the experience of women from different parties, the process of marginalisation, when and how it takes place and how women have responded to it.

Although we relied heavily on secondary material for the historical background of the three parties as well as the background to the issues, the major source of our data were the "histories" of the women themselves and their participation in politics, their struggles within and outside the party, through their own perception of their own potential and the political system's ability or inability to encourage this potential. In order to construct this alternative history as it were, we attempted to reconstruct the real world of politics of these women. In-depth interviews and focused discussions were held with women activists of the three parties both at the Centre and at the State level where these parties were in power (Congress-Madhya Pradesh, BJP-Rajasthan and CPI(M)-West Bengal). The selection of respondents was primarily on the basis of their having either political power (holding office, or being a member of Parliament or Legislative Assembly), or a significant position within the party organisational set-up. At the State level, we also spoke to a number of NGOs concerned, either directly or indirectly, with issues relating to women (Federation of M.P. Women and Child Welfare Agencies, RAHA, Madhya Pradesh, United Front of NGOs Rajasthan, etc.) in order to see the relationship and level of cooperation between political parties and the wider women's movement.

We interviewed almost forty to fifty persons across four States. Interviews of some of the respondents could not be included due to certain objections raised by them. We would have liked to include many more women within the purview of this study but due to the paucity of time and at times sheer inaccessibility of eminent politicians we were forced to restrict the number.

Historical Background 1

The role of women in India, as elsewhere, is defined by their place in history and within the socio-economic system. It has often been pointed out that though women are more equal in the USA in terms of employment opportunities and social status, more women occupy positions of political importance in Europe and Asia. The old societies thus provide a political space in terms of tradition that does not exist in the New World. Given the status of women in these societies this becomes both difficult to understand and accept. It was often overlooked that women in these societies could assume new roles without having to confront or question, ideologically or socially, the basic inequality of the structure in which they found themselves.

Social and Cultural Determinants of Oppression

Indian tradition from Vedic times has been marked by a preference for males over females. Parental craving for the male child is, in part, rooted in the scriptures, which do not allow an individual entry into heaven after death unless his/her last rites are performed by a male child. Religious teachings are, to some extent, responsible for creating and reinforcing customs that contribute to the low status of women in society. Hinduism, the dominant religion in India, teaches young girls to model themselves on Sita, the wife of the mythological hero Rama, who followed her husband into the wilderness and never failed to do his bidding.

Ancient and Medieval India: Manu, the codifier of ancient Hindu law (as mentioned in the *Manu Smriti*, the text of which sets down social codes of conduct for the Hindus)[1] defined the proper societal role of a woman as one in which she is subject to her father in childhood, in youth to her husband, and when her lord is dead, to her sons. Manu's injunctions about the need for protection of women by men at different stages of their lives, have been interpreted to mean 'control by' and 'superiority of' men, while women have been encouraged to be dependent and to lack initiative. Consequently, the family remains the most important influence in the life of a woman, who is usually confined within the four walls of her home. A woman's identity and the course of her life are normally considered to be determined by her husband and his family and, therefore, marriage is the single most determining event in a girl's life. Whatever little political socialisation of women that takes place begins from, and remains confined to, the home and family.

Indian cultural symbols also glorify the woman's role as mother-goddess. She is the symbol of productivity and welfare, spreading happiness and nullifying both wrongs and the wrong-doer. This notion of motherhood has served as an institutionalised form of oppression for the subjugation of women.

Indian cultural symbols also glorify the woman's role as mother-goddess. She is the symbol of productivity and welfare, spreading happiness and nullifying both wrongs and the wrong-doer. She is the divine mother of energy, power and fertility, but this notion of motherhood has served as an institutionalised form of oppression for the subjugation of women. A woman's status is determined by the ability to produce male heirs to perpetuate her husband's lineage, and her identity revolves around the wife/mother roles that negate her individuality. A common characterisation of women in ancient India was as if she were the human counterpart of land,

[1] Coomarswamy, Ananda, *The Dance of Shiva*; Asia Publishing House, Bombay, 1956.

no more than a passive instrument of reproduction. The modern iconography of woman as a nationalist mother-goddess, Bharat Mata, is a particularly interesting variation on the theme, as it elevates the woman to the role of goddess for the goal of nationalism.

The women produced by this society are, quite naturally, affected by the dominant ideology of that society, but this does not completely insulate them against an awareness of its oppression. This awareness, however, has only rarely translated into an agitational consciousness on the part of women; rather, it has more often than not resulted in a feeling of self-alienation amongst them. This is because women are socialised into acceptance of a culture of domination by the male, with the result that the compliance thereof becomes a matter of accepted behaviour and attitude. Women's feelings of anger and alienation have thus historically tended to strengthen, rather than weaken, patriarchal hegemony.

The later periods carried the weight of these premises and were marked by a more visible decline in the status of women, as even while women acquired limited property rights over the years, their overall status in society deteriorated—the age of marriage was lower than before, there was a decline in access to education, widow remarriage was prohibited, and *Sati* became a common practice. Women's status became equivalent to that of the *Shudra*. Around the period of the advent of the Mughal invaders, *purdah* (the veil) became an additional constraint on women. The premium attached to virginity and the social ideal of monogamy contributed to early marriages. During medieval times, the practice of child marriage increased. Once virginity was established as a badge of respectability, it came to be encouraged as a sign of the elite and a measure of belonging to a high caste. Pre-puberty marriages were the order of the day among the Hindus and a further impetus was given to it by making it a matter of social prestige. This practice became so compelling that any departure was received with social disapproval, and considered a matter of social disgrace.

National Movement and Social Reform: The nineteenth century in India witnessed the articulation of specific concerns by social reformers. Basic questions were put forth concerning the discrimination and injustice heaped upon women in Indian society. The impact of the winds of change from the West was clearly manifest in the call for social reform, which was held to be a necessary prerequisite for political evolution. The reform movement (later half of the nineteenth century) was largely built around such issues as *sati* (widow immolation), legalisation of widow remarriage and abolition of *kulin* (upper-caste) polygamy . Represented by most historians as a modern liberal reformer, Raja Rammohan Roy's concern for emancipation of women was considered basic to his wider issues of social reform. It signified the vision of the reformation and the renaissance, and focused on pervasive social evils that were humiliating for society on the whole but for women in particular, since they denied gender dignity and justice to women.

Historians have been perplexed by the gradual disappearance of such issues from the agenda of public debate towards the close of the nineteenth century. From then onwards, the question of the status of women in society did not receive the same attention. The politics of nationalism completely overshadowed any other social concern, and as Partha Chatterjee remarks, "this is surprising, as it was not as if the women's question had been resolved by the social reform movements in Bengal." For Chatterjee, this fact brings into focus two questions. First, could the context of colonialism provide an adequate environment to resolve such issues? Second, what was the relationship between the women's question and the national movement? Chatterjee joins issue with those historians who assume that the West-inspired ideas of social reform in India were a full articulation of liberal values in social institutions and practices, and questions whether such articulation was in fact at all possible in the socio-political conditions created by colonialism. He suggests that the framework in which reform was initiated and its limited agenda was itself inadequate to bring about radical changes in the position of women.

Sumit Sarkar suggests that these efforts at reform may have been a "product of personal necessity" for the new Westernised men, in order to make the necessary interpersonal adjustments within the family. He regards the social movement of the nineteenth century as a failure because it failed to match up to the liberal ideals of equality and reason, caused by the selective adoption of liberal slogans by the reformers and later by the national movement. This view is shared by Chatterjee: "Fundamental elements of social conservatism, such as the maintenance of caste distinctions and patriarchal forms of authority in the family, acceptance of the sanctity of the *shastras* (ancient scriptures), preference for symbolic rather than substantive change in social practices—all of them were conspicuous in the reform movements of the early and mid-nineteenth century."[2]

While there were no previous instances of significant autonomous struggle by women themselves to change relations within or outside the family, it was quite apparent that the reformist movement had significantly altered the lives of women from the days of their mothers and grandmothers. So the question was how this change was to be accommodated within the nationalist project. This was not done by censorship of the reformist agenda, but by resolving the women's question in complete accordance with the preferred goals of the national movement and nationalist ideology, and by separating the domain of culture into two spheres, the material and the spiritual. It was in the material that the claims of Western civilisation were most powerful, as it was held that in order to

2 Chatterjee, Partha, "The Nationalist Resolution of the Women's Question", In *Recasting Women*, (ed.) by K. Sanghari and S. Vaid, 1989, Kali for Women, New Delhi.

counter the colonial powers it is necessary to equip ourselves with Western science and technology. There was no reason however, or so the nationalists held, to imitate the West in every aspect of life as it would threaten the very identity of national cultures. As Chatterjee observes, "what is necessary is to cultivate the material techniques of modern Western civilisation while retaining and strengthening the distinctive spiritual essence of the national culture."[3]

This formed the ideological framework of the nationalist project, and it is a strategy that manifests itself even today—to appropriate from the West all that is material and reject all that is spiritual or ideological. As long as we maintain our spiritual distinctiveness we make all the compromises and adjustment required in the material sphere without losing our identity. This analogy can easily be extended to the outer/inner distinctions. The material is what is outside, it is that which we are forced to adjust to, but ultimately it is not as important as the inner strength of the spiritual world that lies within, which is our 'true self'. Applying the inner/outer distinction to day-to-day existence, we achieve the separation of the social space into *ghar* and *bahir*; *ghar* or the home referring to the spiritual, and *bahir* or the external to the material sphere. The treacherous terrain of material pursuits is external and the vocation of the male, while the home is the bastion of spiritual purity and women are both its representatives as well as its custodians.

Interestingly, this characterisation not only served the objectives of patriarchy, but also of nationalism, as the dichotomy of the material and the spiritual came to acquire another significance in the nationalist mind. The coloniser had been able to colonise the material world but it had failed to colonise the inner spiritual world. It was only in this realm that we were masters of our own fate. Once we match this interpretation with the identification of social roles by gender,

[3] See Sanghari and Vaid, ibid.

we can clearly see how the nationalists resolved the women's issue, as well as salvaged their national pride from subjugation by the colonial masters. It was not merely a question of rejection of the West, but of selection; it was not a dismissal of modernity, but an attempt to make modernity consistent with the nationalist project. And it was this very strategy that was, as Chatterjee observes, "the reason why the issue of women's emancipation disappears from the public agenda of national agitation in the late nineteenth century ... was not because it was overtaken by more emotive issues concerning political power. Rather the reason lies in the refusal of nationalism to make the women's question an issue of political negotiation with the colonial state."[4]

That there was a perception of a threat of Westernisation of Indian women is a fact that can be clearly seen in Bengali literature. The writings of Raja Rammohan Roy and Ishwar Chandra Vidyasagar are marked by some ambiguity of position, but the literature of the second half of the century is unanimous in its rejection (through farces, skits and paintings) of all attempts by Indian women to modernise themselves. The women who attempted to become memsahibs (like English ladies) were ridiculed, their attempts to emulate an English lifestyle of relative leisure combined with a less obsessively caring attitude towards the family was condemned as being out of step with Indian traditions. Quite often this perception of the threat of Westernisation in the realm of values and ideas was compounded with the threat of colonialism itself. From such writings, the new norms for organising family life and determining the right conduct in the conditions of the modern world could be deduced—men would deal with the changes in the material world. Even if the family had to confront changes in the social realm, the essential spiritual quality of the culture had to be maintained and women had to take the main responsibility. No matter what the changes in the external

[4] See Sanghari and Vaid, ibid.

world, women were not to lose their essentially spiritual (feminine) virtues, they were therefore to resist Westernisation. The essential difference between the social roles of men and women, in terms of material and spiritual virtues, had to be maintained.

This conception of the new woman was rooted in a middle-class perception of classical tradition, and it distanced middle-class women from the Western woman as well as women of other classes from their own culture. At the same time, the life of the middle-class woman had changed in the last hundred years. There was a growing need for education, for social acceptability, and therefore education had to be made 'safe' by creating a language and literature suited to the new educated woman. This new literature glorified feminine virtues such as chastity, self-sacrifice, submission, devotion, kindness, and patience. Women also had to have qualities of orderliness, thrift, cleanliness, responsibility and literacy and in order to acquire these, women would have to have some knowledge of the outside world. A woman could venture out into the world as long as it did not endanger her femininity. This made possible the displacement of the boundaries of the home from its purely physical confines, earlier defined by the *purdah* (the seclusion), to a more flexible, but culturally determinate, domain set by the difference between socially approved male/female conduct. This spiritual aspect of her femininity was clearly defined—by her dress, her eating habits, her social demeanour and her religiosity. Thus we see that whatever the sources in the classical religions of India or medieval religious practices, the ideological construct of *Sati-Savitri-Sita* as we know it today is the product of a dominant middle class during the period of the national movement.

The attempt of the reform movement to glorify the role of women thus failed to take up the cause of women's emancipation, since the reforms were restricted by a value system that maintained the essentially derogatory view of women engendered by patriarchal values. However, even though these movements resulted in only a minor change quantitatively, they nevertheless chipped away at the vast oppressive structure that existed. A questioning had begun. As Mazumdar has observed: "The nineteenth century social reform movement was as keen to imbibe Western progressive and democratic values as it was to re-establish the past glory of Indian society. This urge to change and yet to root this change in one's indigenous culture was natural to a society that had experienced the trauma of colonialism. However, this very contradiction influenced to a very large extent the way the woman's question developed subsequently." [5]

Evolution of Women's Organisations: The early twentieth century was marked by an intensification of the national movement. As part of the same process, this period witnessed the emergence of women's organisations – the Women's Indian Association in 1917, the National Council of Women in India in 1926 and the All India Women's Conference (AIWC) in 1927. For these organisations, the major issue was the nature of the relationship between the women's movement and the national movement. This question raised the need for redefinition of women's role in social and public life. Should the women's movement be concerned only with women's issues, or should it also encompass wider political and social concerns? Opinion was divided. While one section felt taking up wider issues would dilute the specific concerns of women, the other argued that colonialism and its oppression had a direct bearing on women's oppression, and only a free India could create the appropriate context for women's freedom. However, as Mazumdar's study of All India Women's Conference of the period[6] demonstrates, the lines were not sharply drawn. But the division could be seen clearly in the debates around particular issues, such as the issue of cooperation with the Simon

5 Mazumdar, ibid.

6 Mazumdar, Vina, *Women's Participation in Political Life in India*, CWDS (Unpublished).

Commission.[7] Certain groups of women wondered whether it would be better to co-operate with the British and get some concessions for women, or whether it was necessary to define the women's struggle as political and against the British. The women's movement in this period held that the current low status of women was an aberration from India's golden past, and was careful not to poach on "the rights of men which were legitimately theirs". These debates made a far-reaching contribution to the now common perception of women's issues as being primarily a welfare or a social question and as having little to do with the nature of government and political development.

Though Gandhi played a crucial role in expanding women's participation in political life, his use of religious symbolism confined them to playing merely a supportive role, based on the example of Sita and Damayanti—women's participation in the national movement was *dharma*.

Though Gandhi played a crucial role in expanding women's participation in political life, his use of religious symbolism confined them to playing merely a supportive role, based on the example of Sita and Damayanti—women's participation in the national movement was *dharma*. But as far as their dignity and their legal rights were concerned, Gandhi was unstinting in his advocacy of absolute equality. And although he was initially against women taking part in any direct political action, he later reversed his decision and encouraged their participation, motivated perhaps more by sheer necessity than choice. Yet, even when the basic issue of women's right to participate in politics was settled, the content of their political role continued to be an open question. The earlier influences of

7 The all-White Simon Commission 1927-28 was appointed by the British Government for the purpose of recommending whether or when responsible Government would be established in India.

cultural nationalism were never completely negated and the women's question continued to be viewed from a middle-class perspective. This prevented any serious analysis of traditional roles or a fundamental questioning of the gendered world-view that prevailed.

Political Equality and Institutions in Independent India

The Committee on the Status of Women in India (CSWI) in its report *Towards Equality* (1975) has clearly demonstrated that the issue of equality of the sexes was never a topic of serious debate in independent India. Based on a study of the proceedings of the Constituent Assembly, party documents, and detailed discussion with party leaders, the CSWI states that the principle was accepted without discussion, but differences emerged as soon as it came to translating the principle of equality into legislation pertaining to laws governing marriage, inheritance and guardianship.

Ideological acceptance of the concept of equality was much higher among the Left Parties in the post-independence era. But even they did little to expand their understanding of the specific needs of women. They assumed that women's development, was a part of the long-term policy for social development and that this could be achieved through education and employment. In the fight for freedom, the Congress had provided an umbrella for different ideological trends that shared the goal of independence. Now that the common goal had been achieved, differences started to emerge, taking the form of conflicting and competing groups. These differences intensified during the debates on development.

Women's organisations increased in number with the increase in political parties. Some of them adopted a policy of collaboration with the government, accepting its assistance to provide the much-needed social services to women and other handicapped sections of society. Such organisations tended to reject organised political action and agitational methods of pressing women's demands before the government and the public. Other groups became increasingly associated with political parties and adopted agitation, confrontation and political action as methods for redressing grievances and getting public attention. Despite the participation of women in both types of movement they neglected to raise women's issues and quite often were led, or guided, by men. As a result, even in the labour movement when the demand for labour legislation for women workers was raised, they did not fight for the rights of women at all levels. This lapse has been acknowledged by more progressive parties and trade union leaders in later years.

Amongst the politically affiliated organisations, the AIWC represents the trend of non-confrontation, while the National Federation of Indian Women (NFIW), which was formed in 1954, represents the more agitational approach despite occasional lapses into a 'welfare orientation' body. Initially, the AIWC was also fairly militant—it fought to get the Hindu Code Bill passed despite stiff opposition in the early years of independence—but in the post-1952 period, it adopted what Mazumdar calls a 'deputationist' approach. Social work and involvement with development work became its major preoccupation, and it concerned itself with issues of health, education, child care and family planning.

Most women who joined the NFIW had been members of the AIWC and many of them had Communist leanings. Its formation was a result of increasing conflict within the AIWC on its scope and function and the group that broke away emphasised that, besides welfare activities, the organisation should develop a social democratic consciousness and be politically active on issues of national and international importance. Many of the organisational questions that members of the NFIW raised after independence later became issues of

One fact that emerges very clearly from most studies on women and political participation is that there was an overall neglect of their aspirations and their need for political participation by both political parties and the government.

debate within the AIWC itself. The fact that the AIWC had such close connections with the Congress, the party in power, always became a limiting factor in the radical positions they could take on different issues and the agitations they could spearhead.

One fact that emerges very clearly from most studies on women and political participation is that there was an overall neglect of their aspirations and their need for political participation by both, political parties and the government.

The Women's Movement and the Post-Emergency Era: There was a perceptible shift in attitude both on the part of the women's movement as well as the government after 1975. This period is marked by the submission of the report by the Commitee on the Status of Women in India (CSIW) set up by government, *Towards Equality*. The most shocking finding of the report was that planned development had added to the misery of women rather then alleviating it. This led to Parliament adopting an unanimous resolution asking the government to mount a "comprehensive legislative and executive action to remove the disabilities and discrimination that Indian women continue to suffer from." Such pressures came along with renewed and growing vigour in the women's movement, marked by increasing protest against discrimination and crime against women. A large number of non-government organisations that emerged and became active during this period had no direct links with political parties. At the same time women's organisations associated with political parties began to assert their demand and fight for the rights of women to independent livelihood and basic resources such as credit, training and technology. Since many of these organisations were affiliated to political parties, the militancy of the women had a considerable impact on the parties, especially those of the Left. Even the non-Left parties, whose leadership was well known for its previous conservative position regarding women's issues, were compelled to start expressing concern for women's rights. The media was also forced to provide coverage to issues related to women. The judiciary became sensitive and started to respond to crimes against women in a more humane way.

It would be interesting to understand why the women's movement was infused with this new spirit. One possible reason could have been that due to the International Decade for Women (1975-85) there was a new awareness among women. Linked to this was the increasing exposure of the movement to Western feminism and feminist debates through the programmes organised during the international women's year. And lastly, there was the growing fund of information brought out by research in the field (the *Towards Equality* Report) revealing the actual condition of women in India. Some researchers have also felt that this new spirit drew heavily on the movements against the Emergency declared by Mrs Gandhi, after the Allahabad High Court verdict setting aside her election on the grounds of electoral irregularities. The most significant development of this period was the people's willingness to articulate their grievances and reassert their democratic rights and it is claimed that the women's movement represented one dimension of this upsurge.

Increasing participation of women was evident both in the formal electoral process and in the popular protests against the deteriorating condition of Indian society (the movement against the Emergency as well as the anti-price rise demonstrations). Although ideologically fragmented into many groups, increasingly there was a tendency among organisations to unite on issues (Muslim Women's Bill, anti-Sati demonstrations)

They were united in their efforts to make the wider polity understand that the question of women's equality was a sexual and not a social one. There was also a growing awareness even among the non-political organisations (e.g., YWCA) of the need for direct political action and concrete political positions on social and political issues.

Despite these developments the current situation is marked by a decline in the sex ratio, high mortality rates, low levels of literacy and employment for women:

Women's Status

	1991	1981	1971
Females per 1,000 Males	927	934	930
Female Workers per 1,000 Male Workers	306	242	181
Literacy Rates in Percentage			
Males	64	54	46
Females	39	28	22

In general, the condition of women has worsened, as the advantages of education, legal rights and changes in social attitudes have become available only to a few privileged sections. And none of this has translated into even a semblance of genuine political equality between Indian men and women. As the CSWI observed in its report *Towards Equality*:

> The right to political equality has not enabled women to play their role as partners and constituents in the political process, because we have forgotten Gandhiji's dictum of not to treat political right as an end in itself but only as a means. Instead these rights have created an illusion of equality and power that is frequently used as an argument to resist special protective and

acceleratory measures to enable women to achieve their just and equal position in society.[8]

An earlier study by the authors[9] confirmed these observations as:

> A recurring question is that despite the increasing participation of women in the voting process, no one has taken the responsibility to inform them of their rights and responsibilities—very few women are members of parties, very few participate or witness political activities like meetings, rallies, campaigning or canvassing. It is only when this base is captured and expanded as a catchment area for women at decision-making levels can they make a significant impact on the political scene. The socialisation at home, the lack of interaction of women with outside developments and the seclusion from political discussions, leaves women devoid of political information and training.[10]

The concern for women's political equality in India first emerged as a political issue during the attempt to transform the freedom movement into a mass movement. Although this movement did yield some sort of equality for an elite class of women, it did not ensure equality on a universal, cross-class level. After independence, too, the situation has yet to change substantially, and even the elite group of women cannot be said to be favoured, as shown by the limited and totally disproportionate representation women have had in Parliament and assemblies. The number of women members in Parliament has rarely gone beyond 10 percent; in fact, there has been a perceptible decline over time. Moreover, the narrow social base of such representatives usually limits the choice to

[8] CSWI, *Towards Equality*, ibid.

[9] Kumari, Abhilasha and Kidwai, Sabina, *Illusion of Power: The Women's Vote*, FES, 1994.

[10] See Kumari and Kidwai, ibid.

family members of influential politicians. This hardly creates a scenario where we can say that the vast majority of women are effectively participating in the democratic process, let alone providing a feminist perspective to the general political thinking.

Increasingly over the past decade, there has been a dissatisfaction with the fact that politics and political assessment have been restricted to the elite class of women politicians created by the nationalist struggle. Attempts have been made to change the situation where "women do not figure as a powerful force in the political decision-making process. Perhaps the reason for this is that they have not recognised themselves as a group which can wield power. Individually women have been completely disempowered. Psychologically they have been socialised into believing the disempowered women is the ideal. In order to legitimise her position she is made the custodian of tradition that confines her."[11]

These reasons have led certain women political activists to believe that male dominated political parties whatever their political position will not accommodate women and have suggested the formation of a 'Women's Political Party'. The formation of a women's political party assumes that all women irrespective of different political hues can, and have, the same political perspective in terms of the kind of goals they seek to achieve and the ways of achieving them. This is perhaps naive, since it would force us to believe that a woman who subscribes to liberal secular politics can sit on the same political platform as one who does not just because they are both women. Political affiliations have to have ideological perspectives, and just by being women we do not necessarily subscribe to the same ideology. Moreover, this exclusionist policy *vis-a-vis* men may actually work against the goals of the platform, since true social change cannot be expected to take place with the participation of only half the population. In fact, proposals like these may be

[11] See Kumari and Kidwai, ibid.

seen to be a retreat and a prevarication, an attempt to avoid confronting the problems directly—the question of women's legitimate participation in the public sphere and of the dismantling of patriarchal control over political parties.

The Indian National Congress 2

Historical analysis reveals that most of the political tendencies within the national movement were in one way or another influenced by the then prevalent discourse of "cultural nationalism". The attitudes that the various political configurations in the freedom struggle displayed towards the women's question were also largely mediated in terms of this discourse, although not without negotiations with the ideological framework into which the discourse was being adopted. If one examines the historical development and ideological premises (as expressed in their electoral rhetoric and manifestos) of the parties that were born of the freedom struggle, one gets a clear indication of their professed positions on the role of women in society as well as their attitude to the question of women's political participation. This created a dilemma for the Left parties as well as for parties like the Congress, because their liberal notions of social justice repeatedly came into direct conflict with accepted notions of Indian culture and women's role in it, which had to be preserved at all costs. The Congress, in order to avoid any such confrontation, ideologically mystified its position on women's issues and ambiguity became the hallmark of their way of dealing with issues raised by women from time to time. This becomes very evident when we look back and see how women were brought into the Congress and the basis on which they were mobilised.

The Genesis

The history of the Congress Party is replete with the names

of great women who rose to prominence, especially during the freedom movement. It is, therefore, not surprising that the Congress takes a certain legitimate pride in the major role it has played in bringing the Indian woman into active politics. However, it must be simultaneously noted that, except for a brief period when the Congress leaders were in jail and the movement was led by Aruna Asaf Ali, these women played a largely subordinate and supportive role. Aruna Asaf Ali stands out as an exception amongst the women of the Congress movement of the time. Having had to defy convention and parental authority in her personal life, she was a militant politician who did not ever completely conform to the Congress's notions of a woman politician.

The Quit India Movement provided an opportunity for women like Aruna Asaf Ali to prove their mettle in violent, secret underground activity as had the earlier terrorist movements.[1] Most of the Congress leadership was in jail during

[1] Unlike the Congress and Gandhi, the militant organisations of the national movement did not try to win women's support and were, in fact, hesitant to include women in their ranks. In conformity with traditional views of women, these organisations thought women could not take the physical and mental strain that they would have to face, but that opinion was soon changed by the aggressiveness and bravery with which women embraced and fought for the cause of freedom. Women excelled themselves in militant nationalist struggles all over the country, proving their courage in active encounters with the British forces. History bears witness to these facts, as recorded in accounts of the attempts on the lives of Governors and other British officials carried out by young girls, students of the University and colleges of Calcutta.

Women members of these militant organisations had to undergo the same kind of training as the men. No special privileges were granted to them, nor was any undue emphasis placed on their being women. Although the fact that the discourse of these militant organisations was replete with the traditional religious imagery when it came to describing women (certainly a drawback of their approach) it is important to realise that even this imagery influenced and helped many women to join the movement. The prime deities were Kali and Durga, deities characterised by violence, aggression and destruction, and therefore signifying characteristics stereotypically associated with men rather than women. This imagery eliminated many conventional arguments against women's participation in violent movements, as it provided an alternate definition of what is feminine. With this imagery, the weakness and passivity arguments could no longer be

the movement and no clear-cut guidelines had been given as to the direction the agitation was to take. Due to this existing uncertainty, a few Congress women (Aruna Asaf Ali, Sucheta Kripalani and others) took the responsibility of directing and organising the masses through sustained secret violent acts. It is now accepted that without such direction the movement would perhaps have collapsed within a few weeks. Gandhi disagreed with Aruna Asaf Ali on the methods employed in the course of the agitation, and while she was ready to consider his advice, she questioned any strategy that would require Indians to submit to the British, as she was in "no mood to surrender to an unrepenting enemy".[2] Aruna Asaf Ali's career represents the growing confidence among women and their burgeoning desire to be independent and to assert their point of view.

The Congress was not prepared to accept this form of struggle, and even Ali was later made to abandon her radicalism once the leadership under Gandhi was back in the saddle. Women were rarely given the opportunity to act on their own initiative, primarily doing what they were told, and never questioning the basic premise of this unequal relationship. Gandhi's support was also important in enabling women to participate in the Non-Co-operation movement, as he made genuine efforts to mitigate the potentially hostile societal reaction to their participation. He protected them from unfavourable comments and insinuations about their respectability. However, it might be that the presence of a protective male authority like Gandhi was not as crucial as it

used to keep women out of politics, since women could be avenging goddesses as well. Moreover, this imagery allayed the fear that every woman who transgresses the boundaries of stereotypical roles feels—that of being termed as unnatural or un-feminine—and legitimised women's venturing out of the domestic space and beyond notions of conventional feminine behaviour both in their own eyes as well as society at large. However, by 1934, most of these secret militant organisations disintegrated.

2 Jawaharlal Nehru Papers, *Elite Women in India Politics*, Letter of Aruna Asaf Ali to Mahatma Gandhi, 1 August 1944.

may now seem—women in the militant movement, which lacked male authority of such stature, did not suffer from any stigma or require any sanction. While there may have been criticism about the nature of their political activity, they commanded personal respect and were praised for their commitment and sacrifice in the context of the national movement.

The Congress, by accepting the need to improve the status of women and by encouraging women in the new role of revolutionaries, emphasised society's commitment to give women the opportunity to participate in all aspects of public and political activity. At the same time, the limited definitions it offered of this equality prevented a genuine debate on women's rights, roles and functions in society from taking place. While Congress politics enabled women to experiment with different roles and to inhabit the public domain, this participation in political activity left the basic structure of society unquestioned and did not generate a far-reaching feminist movement or ideology. Questions raised by Western feminism such as the right to reject the domestic or maternal role, discrimination against the female child, societal definitions of sex-roles, and other related matters were hardly discussed.

Women who were involved in nationalist politics for a time, put aside the conventional definitions of their role in society—definitions that inhibited their mobility and limited them to the home and family. There was, however, no debate on a permanent restructuring of traditional sex roles. Though not explicitly stated, it was recognised that women could participate in politics in a national emergency or in a situation that existed during the anti-colonial struggle. However, in a normal political environment, women's primary responsibility was to the home and family, as politics was considered to be essentially a male prerogative and sphere of activity. This belief was held even by the women who were actively involved in political activity —successful women like Manibehn Patel and Kamaladevi

Chattopadhyay apparently internalised this assessment as they remarked, after a lifetime of political involvement, that a woman's nature is unsuited to political activity.[3]

In personal interviews, most Congress women did not acknowledge any ill-feeling or hostility from their male colleagues; the few who did, traced the men's disapproval to deeply ingrained notions of custom and tradition that did not favour the political participation of women. Mridula Sarabhai asserted that women had to struggle within the Congress to be accepted as independent and responsible colleagues. She suggested that those women who were satisfied with assigned roles were accepted and appointed to important positions, but women like herself who were assertive had to struggle to merely survive within the organisation. So barring a few exceptions, subordination within the party to male leadership was accepted.[4]

The participation of women in the Congress, and more specifically in Gandhian politics, increased steadily throughout the period of national movement, but there was no proportionate increase in women as representatives or delegates to the annual All India Congress Committee (AICC) meetings. In 1922, out of the 350 delegates to the AICC, only 16 were women. Women had made a significant contribution to the 1930 *satyagraha* in terms of mass participation, but the number of delegates to the AICC sessions remained insignificant. In 1930, out of 21 provinces electing 350 members, in all only 8 provinces elected 13 women members. In 1937, of 285 members again only 13 were women. In 1940, the year in which the Women's Department was established, the number dwindled to 5, out of a total of 386, and of these women less than half had played significant roles in either local or national politics.

In 1936-37, when Jawaharlal Nehru as President of the Congress did not appoint a woman to the Working Committee,

3 *Ibid.*

4 *Ibid.*

the incident provoked protests from Mahatma Gandhi. In an address to women's organisations Gandhi remarked:

> I would have welcomed even stronger protests for I wanted our women to be more aggressive and to insist on their rights, both political and social. I invited them to organise themselves to press for their right which they were not likely to get if they waited for the goodwill of their menfolk. [5]

It would be erroneous to surmise that Jawaharlal Nehru did not support the cause of women in politics. He had, on a number of occasions, expressed pride in women who had joined politics and suggested that women should have the freedom to choose from a wide variety of roles and not be confined to the role of wife, mother and homemaker. However, it is important to realise that this contradiction between word and deed continued in Congress politics. Most men within the Congress did not think that women were good enough to share power and responsibility and many appointments of women to positions of office did not significantly change their positions within their party.

Mobilisation of the Elite Women

There was no serious attempt to politically educate and bring the broad mass of women into active politics. Gandhi recruited women from the families of his colleagues and associates to provide leadership to the group of women in politics. Despite the fact that these women of elite status may have been chosen for their ability, involvement and commitment to nationalism, they cannot, either as delegates to Congress meetings or as members of the Working Committee, be considered representative of the masses of women who were involved in nationalist politics. The women who were politically

[5] *Elite Women in India Politics*, Letter written by Mahatma Gandhi to Jawaharlal Nehru on 29 May 1936.

successful fell into two categories: (a) those with family affiliations to the Congress and its leadership, and (b) those from wealthy and progressive families, with the first group tending to dominate in numbers. For example, at the AICC session of 1922, 9 out of the 16 women delegates fell into this first category: 3 of them were from the Nehru household; the 2 delegates from Bengal were the wife and sister of C.R. Das; and the 2 Muslim women were Mohammed Ali's mother and Hasrat Mohani's wife, Sarladevi Chaudharani, Rabindranath Tagore's niece and wife; of a politically active lawyer in Punjab, Rambhug Chowdhary; and the ninth, Kamaladevi Chattopadhyay, was married to Sarojini Naidu's brother, although her political career cannot really be said to have derived from any influence other than that of her own efforts and commitment. In 1937, out of the 8 women members, 6 were well known, the newcomers being Satyawati, the granddaughter of Swami Shradhananda, and Mridula Sarabhai, the daughter of the textile magnate, Ambalal Sarabhai.

A few of the women who assumed leadership roles in the nationalist movement, had entered politics due to some personal tragedy. The most frequent causes were an unhappy marriage and early, or child, widowhood (Anusuyabehn Sarabhai, Kamaladevi Chattopadhyay, Lilavati Munshi, etc.). These women, in their personal crises, had not followed the lifestyle traditionally sanctioned as appropriate to their situation, but had chosen an unconventional and unusual means of coping with it. Their choice put them outside the framework of conventional and orthodox society. As 'deviants' they were no longer restricted or limited to structured sex roles.

Many women also joined the freedom movement in support of their husbands or other family members. Basanti Devi, the wife of C.R. Das, became active with the support of her husband and her involvement came to an end with his death. Sucheta Kripalani was only marginally involved in politics before her marriage to J.B. Kripalani, her political career beginning in earnest after her marriage. Muslim women followed this course as well—Mohammed Ali's mother and wife became involved in politics only after his arrest. The presence of Hindu women in politics persuaded Muslim nationalists to encourage similar participation among their women.

Unlike Gandhi and Nehru, Mohammad Ali Jinnah did not attempt to mobilise the support of women at public meetings during the national movement. He, however, encouraged close female associates to be politically active and indirectly influenced the attitude of women. He would ask his sister to sit on the speaker's platform with him. Begum Ikramullah suggests that the presence of Ms. Jinnah encouraged many Muslim women to join political meetings as they no longer felt anxious about being targets of orthodox Muslim opinion.

The success of these women, and of those who lacked political affiliations prior to their entry into politics, was a result of the efforts made by reform movements throughout the nineteenth and early twentieth centuries to improve the position of women. Liberal and progressive families and reform associations were committed to eliminating the serious and systematic injustice against women in the social, educational and political realms. These women politicians were socialised in such families and in an environment sensitive to social change. This frequently involved membership of reform societies like the Brahmo Samaj or Arya Samaj. Membership of these societies required accepting the importance of women's right to education, marriage at a decent age (defined as teenage), and the right of women to attend public meetings along with men. Women who belonged to such families, were relatively free from the rigid structure of sex-roles and could adopt new lifestyles. These families were sensitive to the changes being introduced in the lives of upper-class women, and they did not expect the lives of their women members to conform to the traditional values and patterns set by society. Nevertheless, women's participation in politics was conceived within a framework that gave importance to their roles as wives and mothers, and the main difference from the traditional Hindu thinking lay in the perception of the political role as something that did not exclude the traditional ones. Women who were active politicians in this period, thus, did not choose between tradition and politics; rather, they were required to combine the two. On the other hand, a woman's traditional capacity to sacrifice was especially emphasised by Gandhi in an effort to mobilise women. Her capacity to sacrifice her own personal interest for the family was held to extend to the community and nation, and this motivated women to join the Non-Cooperation Movement.

A woman's traditional capacity to sacrifice was especially emphasised by Gandhi in an effort to mobilise women. Her capacity to sacrifice her own personal interest for the family was held to extend to the community and nation, and this motivated women to join the Non-Cooperation Movement.

Leadership of the Elite

Elite women members of the Congress were consciously directed to embody the commitment that Congress leaders felt towards social change. Women leaders were given the responsibility of projecting their life and new roles as symbols of political commitment in order to motivate women from other classes to emulate them. The critical status of these women was expected to strengthen the resolve of other women leaders to be successful in public and political careers. The fact of the matter, however, was that these women could serve as models only for the middle and lower-middle classes, as the opportunities that were available to elite women were exclusive and restricted to their social group. Women from the lower classes had limited access to positions of power and authority and had little direction and knowledge of the fundamentals of political life. The status and prestige acquired by elite women during the Nationalist Movement cannot therefore be generalised to apply to all women in Indian society. They were the exceptions and do not indicate a new direction or expanding opportunities for all classes of women.

A significant factor in the careers of the women politicians, was the support and patronage of Congress leaders, although this does not necessarily negate their individual merit or their ability to hold responsible positions. The nature of this relationship, however, had a significant impact on their success, appointment or access to political office. The power, prestige and responsibility of women politicians was exaggerated and exploited to publicise the liberated attitude of Indian society. Moreover, a comparison of the basic political attributes—such as independence, ability to initiate and organise movements and a political power base—of Sarojini Naidu, Sucheta Kripalani and Kamaladevi Chattopadhyay reveals that success, or appointment to political office was dependent generally on the guidance of Mahatma Gandhi rather than on actual capability. Women politicians who functioned independently of Gandhian guidance had limited success. Kamaladevi Chattopadhyay had taken her cause to the masses by campaigning for the peasants, and was one of the leading figures of the Congress Socialist Party. Her political base, however limited, was real. But if measured by the importance of political office, Sucheta Kripalani and Sarojini Naidu were more successful.

Those women who became prominent on the national or provincial level shared amongst them common characteristics of wealth, education, power and status. The interaction of these factors differed in individuals; some were more wealthy than educated, others had education but little status. To this was added kinship connections, and the patronage of Congress leaders. These attributes have been more or less trendsetters for what followed in the post-independence period.

Post-Independence Dilemmas

The Hindu Code Bill: The Congress was completely divided on the issue of the Hindu Code Bill just after independence, and stalwarts like Pattabhi Sitaramayya, president of the Congress, the then President of India Rajendra Prasad, Sardar Patel and many other prominent Congress leaders vociferously opposed it. For the first time they were faced with a situation when women's rights confronted established tradition. Women members of Parliament, on the other hand, fresh from the strength and confidence of having actively contributed to the freedom struggle were united across party lines in demanding reform. This was referred to by members of Parliament as a "tyranny of women". Every clause of the Bill was vehemently opposed, including the one that abolished polygamy, and specially the one that gave female offspring inheritance rights in ancestral property.[6] Members in Parliament called the Bill "anti-Hindu and anti-Indian", and the cry of "religion in danger" resounded through the country. Massive demonstrations against the Bill were staged in different parts of the country and outside Parliament. The Bill was first introduced in 1944 but could not be passed until 1955. By the time the Bill was passed it had been amended so many times that it gave women only limited benefit.

In today's context, we often fail to appreciate the struggle these women waged for even minor concessions from the conservative and patriarchal males who dominated the party. The controversy around the Hindu Code Bill presents a historical lesson for the women's movement today in that it demonstrates the struggle needed to reform any religious law. Even today, any reform in religious laws is met with stiff resistance. For instance, the recent attempt by the Andhra Pradesh State Legislature to amend the Hindu Succession Act

6 Because of this opposition, in the final version of the Bill, daughters were denied this right.

and make daughters co-partners in joint family property came in for a lot of criticism and was delayed because of opposition by the ruling party at the Centre.

Plans and Policies

The Congress, as the leader of the freedom struggle, formed the first government in independent India. Since then, the Congress has been ousted out of power only thrice, and it has initiated a number of programmes aimed at improving the status of women. Thus from the very beginning the Congress Government of independent India was committed to implementing the basic structural changes needed to improve the lot of women in society as envisaged by the first National Planning Sub-committee and the Directive Principles of State Policy. However, the form these changes took in the Five Year Plans did not fulfil these expectations. With the exception of the Second Five Year Plan, all other plans confined their concerns to education, health and welfare.

The period of Nehruvian Socialism with its attendant emphasis on development programmes came to an end in the sixties which had made little focused attempt to improve the lot of women. A split in the party and the emergence of Congress(I) under Mrs. Indira Gandhi brought about changes in the ideology of the Congress. The seventies and eighties marked a crucial period of change. The declaration of Emergency which led to an erosion of democratic values was followed by a struggle for the restoration of democracy. The fall of Mrs. Gandhi, the 1984 riots and the subsequent rise of Rajiv Gandhi are events which brought about a major change in the secular democratic traditions of the Congress.

The era of Rajiv Gandhi was significant in the launch of many welfare schemes for women and also the tabling of the motion for 33 per cent reservation for women in *panchayats*. It has also been acknowledged by most Congress women that the Mahila Congress was at its best during this period as Rajiv consciously encouraged women's participation.

Programmes for women and children received an unprecedented boost in the Five Year Plans during the Rajiv Gandhi period. For the first time, a major exercise was initiated to prepare a detailed perspective plan for the social, economic and political advancement of women, both in the organised sector and among the self-employed women. The National Perspective Plan for Women is aimed at empowering women and enabling them to be recognised and rewarded in a measure commensurate with their role in nation-building. The National Commission on Women was also established during this period and a Commissioner appointed for women's rights to promote the social well-being of women.

However, if we were to make an overall evaluation of Congress' performance *vis-a-vis* women, it is marked by a lack of clear perspective on the role and status of women in today's society, and welfarism is seen as a substitute for real solutions to social problems that oppress women. Even when meaningful policies have been formulated they were not effectively implemented and have failed to change the lot of women. The Committee on the Status of Women in India points out quite clearly that the government has failed to integrate women's needs as equal citizens in programmes for agricultural and industrial development. This can be seen by the absence of any effort on the part of the government to generate and improve women's employment. On the contrary, the neglect of their productive role has caused large-scale displacement of women from the labour force. This could not be offset by the marginal increase of women in the service sector and in white-collared jobs, although the visibility of a certain class of women in these spheres has created the illusion of substantial gain.

Having recognised their failure in the sphere of policy and implementation, the government has now shifted the onus of dealing with issues of social inequality on non-government agencies and, as Mazumdar points out, is content to play merely a supportive role.

Women's Rights and Political Imperatives

The ambivalent attitude of the Congress (I) in articulating and pursuing a progressive policy on women and women's rights in the post-independence period, and especially in the 1980s, is best illustrated by two important events. One was the Shah Bano judgement and the subsequent passing of the controversial Muslim Women's Protection of Rights on Divorce Act of 1986. The second was the *sati* incident at Deorala in 1987. Both these events generated a great deal of controversy, and various political parties took contrary stands in keeping with both their differing ideologies and self-perceived vote banks. Protests by Congress (I) women MPs were only on an individual level, as the party followed a policy of communal pacification. The most significant aspect of these events, however, was the widespread reaction on the part of women's organisations and the inability of Congress women to change the parties' opportunistic and reactionary line.

The status of women under the Muslim Personal Law was brought to the fore in April 1985, when Justice Chandrachud (then Chief Justice of Supreme Court) passed a judgement directing the payment of Rs 179. 20 as maintenance to Shah Bano by her ex-husband. Under the provisions of the Muslim Personal Law, the husband had to pay maintenance to his divorced wife for only three months after the divorce, or what is known as the *iddat* period. A huge uproar followed the judgement, as the fundamentalist elements within the Muslim community challenged it as violating their Personal Law, even while the media and the progressive intelligentsia hailed it as a landmark judgement. Historic it certainly was, since it brought the issues of the validity of Personal Law and minority rights to the centre-stage of Indian politics, and the events that followed this judgement contributed in no mean terms to the further communalisation of Indian politics and the rise of Right-wing Hindu fundamentalism.[7]

The judgement led to a complete polarisation within the Muslim community. On the one hand were reformists and liberals who acclaimed the Supreme Court judgement for giving the much-needed relief and security to Muslim women. But the orthodox elements in the Muslim community felt that it was a wrong interpretation of the Koran. Huge demonstrations were held against the Supreme Court judgement on the grounds that it interfered with the Muslim Personal Law and constituted an immense threat to the independent religious identity of Indian Muslims. Consequently, the Congress (I) Government led by Rajiv Gandhi, which had initially supported the judgement, succumbed to the pressure of the conservative elements within the Muslim community and introduced the infamous Muslim Women (Protection of Rights on Divorce) Act 1986. This Act sealed the fate of thousands of women who

[7] In 1978, Shah Bano, a housewife from Indore, approached the judicial Magistrate asking for a maintenance allowance of Rs 500 per month (the maximum amount allowed under Section 125 of the Criminal Procedure Code (CrPc)). Her husband, Ahmad Khan, she alleged, had driven her out of her home, had favoured his second wife and denied her even clothes and medicines. Ahmad Khan, on his part, said that he had divorced Shah Bano by the irrevocable method of saying "talaq, talaq, talaq" and that he was under no obligation to provide further. The Magistrate ordered Ahmad Khan to pay a small sum of Rs 25 per month to his wife. The High Court of Madhya Pradesh later increased this amount to Rs 179. 20 per month. Ahmad Khan then approached the Supreme Court, challenging this order. His main argument was that the payment of maintenance up to the end of the *iddat* period, as well as the *mehr* amount (dower fixed at the time of marriage) concluded the responsibilities of the husband under the Muslim Personal Law.

The Supreme Court rejected his appeal. The judge quoted verses from the Koran to "show that there is an obligation on Muslim husbands to provide for their divorced wives" and dismissed Ahmad Khan's appeal. The court, on the basis of a progressive interpretation of the Shariat, decreed that destitute Muslim divorcees were entitled to maintenance from their husbands, that the husband's responsibility was not limited to the *iddat* period and *mehr.* It also further ruled that in case of any conflict between Sections 125 and 127, of the Criminal Procedure Code (CrPc) and the Muslim Personal Law (MPL) the former would prevail.

were henceforth denied the right to ask for maintenance from their husbands beyond the three-month *iddaṭ* period. The events that ensued made it clear that at least some of the political parties involved, especially the Congress (I), sacrificed the rights of women at the altar of political expediency and ambition, and went down on their knees to communal and reactionary forces.

Once the Prime Minister Rajiv Gandhi chose to support the conservative opinion, all avenues for discussion of the question within the party were immediately closed. Not a single Congress (I) Muslim leader or women's organisation was consulted in arriving at this decision—not even Abida Ahmad or Najma Heptullah, who were active Congress(I) members. Nor was any Muslim or non-Muslim woman of the Opposition consulted. The Union Law Minister, Asoke Sen, defended the Bill as a response to a demand of the majority of Muslims, maintaining that the government had arrived at its decision only after consulting all Muslim leaders. Margaret Alva (Congress (I)) was amongst those who voiced her strong objections, and Rajendra Kumari Bajpai was another Minister who was extremely unhappy, but Mohsina Kidwai (Congress (I)), however, played it safe by adopting a totally ambivalent stand. Ultimately all had to obey the party whip that was used to get the Bill passed.

Rajiv Gandhi strongly defended the Muslim Women (Protection of Rights on Divorce) Bill in the Lok Sabha maintaining that Section 125 of the Criminal Procedure Code was "not giving adequate protection to women". He said that the Bill was "secular, as bringing in the personal law of any religion does not reduce our secularism in any way". He also insisted that the Bill did not deprive divorced Muslim women of maintenance rights but gave them much more than was available under Sections 125 and 127 of the Criminal Procedure Code, although he failed to elaborate how. He declared that under the Indian Constitution secularism is the "right of every religion to coexist with another religion. We acknowledge this by allowing religion to have its own secular laws".[8] In other words, the Rajiv Gandhi Government aligned itself to communal and obscurantist elements in the Muslim community, allowing for further suppression of women.

Women's organisations who strongly opposed the Bill, especially the All India Democratic Women's Association (AIDWA), which has close links with the CPI (M)) maintained that the Bill was not secular, but retrogressive as it sought to take away the minimal rights given to the Muslim divorcee by the Supreme Court. It was anti-women as it sought to make Muslim women second-class citizens by taking away their option to appeal under secular laws. Women lawyers involved in the campaign emphasised that Section 125 does not compel a woman to seek justice from the court. She is still free to go the *qazi* if she so wishes. The women's organisations protested that the Bill had once again put the Muslim woman in the dock and placed the onus of defence on her, leaving her at the mercy of *mullahs* or *qazis* whose views are conservative, oppressive and traditional.

After the passage of the Bill, a delegation consisting of representatives of the All India Association, National Federation of Indian Women (NFIW), Committee for Protection of Rights of Muslim Women (Delhi and West Bengal), Muslim Satyasodhak Mandal (Pune) and the Muslim Women's Rights Protection Committee met the Prime Minister. Rajiv Gandhi rejected their demand for withdrawal of the Muslim Women's Bill. A press release issued by the AIDWA said that he dismissed their plea for equal rights for women and maintenance to divorcees on the ground that these were "Western" and "not Indian" concepts. But he had no answer when countered by the statement that even `parliamentary democracy' was a Western concept. They realised that, for the Congress (I) Government, representatives of the Muslim

[8] *The Telegraph*, 28 February 1986.

community meant only conservative menfolk. The thousands of Muslim women who protested in the streets were not given a hearing. The 13-hour debate in Parliament on the Bill brought out two stark facts—that the present leadership had completely false and dangerous notions of secularism, and that members of the Congress (I) were totally without conscience as far as their concern for the plight of Muslim women was concerned. Influenced by a whip which they dared not defy, all—including women MPs—ended up voting for the Bill.

The Opposition, especially the CPI(M) (with the exception of course of such elements as the Muslim League, the National Conference of Kashmir and Syed Shahabuddin of the Janata), tried their best to persuade the Congress (I) members to act according to their conscience and reject the Bill. Pointing out the dangers inherent in this "unconstitutional, un-Islamic, anti-woman, anti-human" Bill, the Opposition members, tried to mobilise Congress members. Realising that the Bill could be defeated in the House only with their support, they urged the treasury-benches to act with courage and oppose the Bill and the "whip". Far from extending a positive response to this demand, even the Congress (I) members who had earlier opposed the Bill, now rallied together in extolling its so-calledvirtues.

It is interesting to note that during the entire debate on the Bill there was no attempt to defend it as being pro-woman or even secular. A not-so-subtle attempt was made to emphasise that it had been framed in deference to the wishes of the majority of Muslims, and if it was regressive then this was because the majority of Muslims wanted it so. It was also implied that the government was acting in accordance with its definition of secularism, namely, "non-interference in any religion". The government had no choice but to bring in the Bill when certain laws (Section 125 of the Criminal Procedure Code) were perceived by the Muslim community as being tantamount to interference with their Personal Law. The onus of not wanting change was thus laid squarely at the door of Muslims who, it was implied, were inherently conservative thereby ignoring a fairly large section of Muslims which had held rallies, seminars and conventions against the Bill.

The Congress party was also in power in the State of Rajasthan at the time of the *sati* incident (it will be discussed in greater detail in the chapter on Rajasthan) in Deorala in 1985, and the party's response clearly shows it is ideologically not at all clear or equipped to take a position when confronted with tradition, and ultimately its decisions are motivated by political opportunism in response to, and depending on, the amount of pressure different groups can bring to bear on the government. The *sati* incident is also a clear example of how religious sanction can be used to legitimise retrogressive cultural practices, especially those directed against women. The Hindu woman in this case became a symbol reinforcing the Hindu identity and the need to go back to Hindu traditions and beliefs. As a result in both the cases the Congress ended up supporting religious fundamentalism, thus negating women's democratic rights. The party during the 1980s vacillated from the right to the left in accordance with its political ambitions, even while purporting to project a secular, socialist ideological image. Today, this vacillation of the Congress (I) is perceived as blatant opportunism, and it has put the party in a difficult position, with many holding it responsible for the erosion of India's secular traditions and increase in anti-women practices.

These two events are a clear indication of the similarity of views among fundamentalists (irrespective of religion) towards women. The question of maintenance for Muslim women was seen as an onslaught against the Muslim community itself, an attack on the Muslim identity. Similarly, the *Sati* issue accelerated into a question of Rajput identity, and a perception that Hinduism was in danger. The sharp polarisation of views created two definite camps—one communal, the other secular. The Personal Law became an integral part of the political debate and also a major women's issue.

The Nineties : A Party in Ideological Crisis

Thus, the grave injustice done by the Congress by bending backwards to please the communal forces has greatly harmed women's demand for their rights and encouraged the revival of obstructionist and retrograde forces. During the recent elections of 1996 it was found that the Congress continued its policy of vacillation and political opportunism. In spite of progressive promises in the election manifestos, nothing had changed in essence from the days of the national movement. The professed aims of equality, empowerment (social, political and economic) were never seen in the context of its impact either on tradition or social order. It was assumed that women could be freed from bondage with social welfare programmes without having to question any traditional arrangements. Confronting tradition or accepted social values was always seen in the context of vote banks, which no party—especially the party in power—was willing to risk losing.

Even organisational functioning had not really changed much from the old days, the same criteria of connections either of family or wealth, or personal or familial tragedy, determined the allocation of tickets. Tickets were allotted to women like Alka Kamal Nath, Chhabila Netam, who were mere housewives till yesterday and who have entered politics primarily to keep the seat warm for their husbands who could not contest the elections themselves due to the allegations against them in the Jain *hawala* scam.

Media reports during the 1996 elections revealed that Alka Nath was a candidate with virtually no identity—in fact, no one was quite sure what she looked like since she was commonly perceived to be a proxy candidate for her husband, and she admitted as much in the course of the campaign: "I am here to ask for votes for Kamal Nath, who is your actual political representative, and shall remain so in future as well. I can at best be a social activist, a role that I have been performing since 1980 when Kamal Nath was elected from here for the first time." In fact, to ensure that she received the votes intended for Kamal Nath her name on the ballot paper was changed from Alka Nath (as in the list of candidates released by the Congress(I) to Alka Kamal Nath. However, one cannot dispute the fact that the Congress fielded more women candidates than any other party. Sixteen women won the election on the Congress ticket out of the 47 who contested.

At the same time, the Congress has women leaders like Mamata Banerji who because of her aggressiveness is perceived by many Congressmen as a liability that they are forced to carry because of the groundswell of support for her in her constituency, south Calcutta. A survey conducted by Timespoll and Mode[9] showed that a lot of this support comes from her own personal standing and her image as a fighter for the cause she believes in.[10] Known as the single force that has put the Marxists in West Bengal on the defensive, Mamta Bannerji has the reputation of an indomitable rebel, standing against the policies of the ruling Left Front as well as against corruption within the Bengal Congress (I). She is also known as a shrewd manipulator of publicity to generate public sympathy—for example, at the onset of elections she disagreed with nominations put forward by the Bengal Congress (I), claiming that they were criminals, and threatened to go on a hunger strike and withdraw her candidature if she was not allowed her way. Banerji won a spectacular victory in her constituency in 1991 and then again in 1996 but she has been accused of playing the politics of opportunism. Women and women's rights do not figure anywhere on her agenda. Her main plank is her war with the Left Front Government in West Bengal.

The Congress(I) has also within its ranks other women who

9 *The Times of India*, 28 April 1996.

10 *Ibid.*

have worked for their place in the political structure like Girija Vyas, Kumari Selja and Margaret Alva, etc., but the grassroots-level women activists are a rare sight in the corridors of power and due to their small number, the former have failed to have an effective say in the functioning of the party. In spite of the promises held out by the liberal tradition of the Congress party and its stated commitments (in its party documents and policy formulations) to a betterment of the status of women, in all spheres the picture in reality continues to be dismal.

In spite of the promises held out by the liberal tradition of the Congress party and its stated commitments (in its party documents and policy formulations) to a betterment of the status of women, in all spheres the picture in reality continues to be dismal.

3 The Congress Women behind the Movement

For the first time, as we interviewed women politicians, we could almost see history coming to life. All that we had found out from our review of literature began to be translated into actual events with real actors. Our interviews of women like Hamida Habibullah who have had a long association with the Congress party, made it evident that most women who joined the Congress belonged to influential political families. Many of them had struggled and formed a niche for themselves, but even then many of them could not express solidarity with other women struggling for political power, or generate concerted action on women's issues. They faced the discrimination in allotment of tickets, in organisational positions and in holding government offices. Each person's experience is in itself a revelation of the struggles faced by these women individually to survive in an hostile environment . The Congress, more than any other party, carried with it the romance of the independence struggle, at the same time, it also carried post-independence disillusionment specially among veterans such as Begum Hamida Habibullah.

Hamida Habibullah belongs to that generation of Congress loyalists who have been associated with the freedom struggle. Born into an elite Muslim family she received good education but was not politically active until the 1960s. She was greatly influenced by the Gandhi family. Once she joined politics she became an active parliamentarian and her association of two decades with the Congress gave us valuable insight into the politics of that party.[1]

Much of Habibullah's fervour and enthusiasm was based on nostalgia of going back to the National Movement and exposure to luminaries of that time such as Sarojini Naidu and Jawaharlal Nehru. She told us, "When I was 10-12 years of age, I heard Sarojini Naidu at a function at Hyderabad and I was greatly inspired by her. She was talking about the importance of woman's role in building the country. It is important to remember that Hyderabad was a State (kingdom) ruled by the *Nizam* (like a king) and also pro-British. I was studying in an Anglicised school with very proper English teachers where the mere mention of Mahatma Gandhi was considered an act of indiscipline. After the visit of Sarojini Naidu I was greatly inspired and secretly started talking about Mahatma Gandhi. I was caught and reprimanded by my teachers. Once I was married to General Habibullah, I got involved with the social work in schools, training centres for girls, etc. After Independence we got posted to a number of places and I worked towards rehabilitating Sikh refugees from Pakistan in Shillong."

"In 1952, we were posted at the National Defence Academy at Kharakvasla and Jawaharlal Nehru came to visit the Academy accompanied by Mrs Gandhi and her children. I attended all Panditji's meetings and was drawn towards the Congress. In 1965 we returned to Lucknow and I visited my village of Barabanki. The plight of the villagers was unbearable and they asked me to become their MLA (Member of Legislative Assembly). I was greatly encouraged by Begum Anis Kidwai, a freedom fighter and a Congress member of long standing. She, on my behalf, spoke to the Congress President Ajit Prasad Jain to permit me to fight elections. But my enthusiasm was frowned upon, as most of the Congress politicians were *nawabs* and *zamindars*, belonging to the feudal order and were not really interested in doing anything for the people."

1 Habibullah has today retired from active politics and heads the Indian Council for Child Welfare.

"Finally it was only in 1969, only after the split in the Congress[2] that I was given Haidargarh to contest from.. It was a weak constituency for the Congress and the Chief Minister said sarcastically that 'after doing social work in the army I was going to dabble in politics, so this constituency was fine for me'. I was given only Rs. 2000 and told to go and fight an election. My main support and encouragement came from Begum Anis Kidwai. My husband, even though he was pro-Communist, also supported me and we both took it up as a challenge. In spite of opposition by rival groups from within the Congress, with the help of Shanti, a grassroots-level woman activist, I toured the constituency. It was during these tours that I realised the acute lack of sanitation and health facilities in the area. I did face character assassination like most women who enter politics but I finally won the election and became an MLA."

Habibullah feels that the attitude towards women within the party was consistently hostile. "The majority of the men within the party were always working to remove women. Some men were friendly but they were insecure and were afraid that the women would stand up to them. Moreover, there was a very strong hold of men over their wives even after they entered politics and won elections, and they wielded power through them."

Like many of the women politicians of that era who came to the Congress because of the influence of the Nehru-Gandhi family, Hamida Habibullah was a great admirer of Indira Gandhi, although unlike the politicians of today, when she felt her idol was in the wrong she did not hesitate to tell her. She fondly recalls, " I had a great deal of faith in Mrs Gandhi while I held the post of Minister of State for Social Welfare, Civil Defence and National Integration and also while I was a Rajya-

2 Between Indira Gandhi and Morarji Desai on the Bank nationalisation issue. The U.P. Chief Minister S. B. Gupta who belonged to the old guard supported Morarji Desai in his anti-Bank nationalisation stand and hence had to resign.

Sabha member. I was always a supporter of Mrs Gandhi and supported her through all crises. I helped Mrs Gandhi during the contest between Sanjeeva Reddy and V. V. Giri for Presidentship."[3] At the same time, she admits that "Mrs Gandhi was very authoritative and could not perceive anybody as equal to herself. She would not allow any person to go against her decisions and would not allow anybody who could be a threat to her to come up. This was apparent as she never allowed any competent women to acquire any position of real power. When she removed Bahuguna in 1976, I went to her, requesting her to reconsider her decision as he was controlling Uttar Pradesh (UP) very effectively at that time. For the first time I realised that Mrs Gandhi did not like to be contradicted. She was extremely hostile and angry."

"Another incident occurred when I complained that Sanjay Gandhi should not be allowed to interfere with the Family Planning Programme. She was once again very angry and said that Sanjay was the one who was drawing the youth towards us, otherwise they would go with the JP movement.[4] She felt that the Congress would win hands down in the coming election in 1977. Her self-confidence was high and she was surrounded by people who only propped her up and were 'yes-men'. The Congress lost the elections and I continued in the Rajya Sabha. Those of us who did not support the Emergency were told to shut up; she killed freedom of thought and expression."

"The real change for women came during Rajiv Gandhi's time when the Mahila Congress was formed at various district levels. There was a great deal of money spent and it was active in various programmes. The Mahila Congress did exist during

[3] Mrs Gandhi wanted V. V. Giri to be the President, but Sanjeeva Reddy was the party's official candidate. So she asked Congress men and women to vote according to their conscience thereby disobeying the party whip. After the presidential elections, Mrs Gandhi emerged strong and at the helm of the Congress(I).

[4] Mr Jaiprakash Narain, a veteran freedom fighter and Socialist led an anti-corruption campaign against the Congress Government and was able to mobilise a large section of the youth (1974).

Mrs Gandhi's time but she never allowed any other woman to come up. During the time of Rajiv Gandhi, women's issues were raised and discussed. He realised the need for upliftment of women. The *Panchayati Raj* idea was proposed. During the Muslim Women's Bill issue I felt that Rajiv Gandhi was ill-informed, but we had to all obey the party whip. I was the President of the Mahila Congress during Rajiv Gandhi's time and the organisation was very active but now it no longer has the same momentum and enthusiasm. Maybe because it is not receiving the same encouragement from the leadership."

Habibullah has today retired from active politics and heads the Indian Council for Child Welfare. This decision was due to the fact that "in 1985 I did not get a ticket from Haidargarh despite the large amount of work I had done there. After this humiliation I decided to move away from the political arena. Today the Congress is facing an ideological crisis, as there is no cohesive party ideology and functioning. In fact, we at the Indian Council for Child Welfare and the National Commission for Women are doing much better work than any organisation of the Congress party."

Responding to the question of 33 per cent reservation for women in Assemblies and Parliament, she says initially she was hesitant, "I was against reservation of any kind. I always felt that education, food, and all basic necessities should be provided to the weaker sections in order to allow them to come up in life. But reservation at professional levels brings down the standard. However, in the case of women this issue is more complex as they are bound to the domestic sphere and society does not allow them to move up. Reservation seems to be the only option as *Panchayati Raj* elections have proved."

Girija Vyas, President of the Mahila Congress began her career in academics teaching at an American university. She was not interested in politics initially although her father Shri Krishna Sharma had been a freedom fighter and an active politician. Vyas entered politics in support of Mrs Gandhi when she was defeated in 1977. "I joined politics as the President of the district level Congress in Udaipur, working mainly with women. A small women's cell was formed which represented the Mahila Congress at the district level. Initially, the women who joined were women from political families and the main aim was to rebuild the image of Mrs Gandhi." In her commitment to Mrs Gandhi as the leader, when compared to women like Habibullah, Vyas represents a perceptible shift in the way women activists perceived their role in the Congress. From a position of critical commitment to party ideology and leadership of the earlier Congress women, unquestioning devotion to individual leaders becomes the norm, which equates ideological commitment with political commitment to the leader. In such a view, the (woman) activist does not consider important the policies and the ideology of the leader or her frequently authoritarian functioning, only responding emotionally to her defeat. And, if there was to be a restoration of prestige, that restoration was not of the image of the Congress but that of Mrs Indira Gandhi.

At the same time, Vyas recognises that, "during the period of Mrs Gandhi's rule, women did not have significant power and it was during the period of Rajiv Gandhi's tenure that some power came back to women. During Mrs Gandhi tenure, independence of the States deteriorated and all power got centred in the Centre. She was all powerful and the strength of the mafia and money was important in politics. This further affected the participation of women." Furthermore, she also maintained that although the Congress always gave the maximum seats to women, the political affiliation of the family and contacts with party leaders were crucial for getting a ticket. She also admitted that the Congress party had rarely witnessed protests by women MPs against unfair treatment. Like Habibullah, she also felt that the greatest incentive to women came under Rajiv Gandhi's rule when various programmes for women were launched and important posts

> The problem is that women parliamentarians do not work enough to prop other women.

were given to women.

Vyas also noted that, in general, women's issues were rarely supported by women parliamentarians and there was no attempt to unite across party lines on such issues. The causes for this apathy she felt are many: "When I joined politics I was highly educated, I had certain advantages, but I faced discrimination from colleagues. Women are not allowed to speak, there is character assassination, and one has to struggle. Women who are successful are normally given soft Ministries like education, social welfare, women and child. I was the first woman to get a Ministry like taxation, earlier reserved for men. Social conservatism is enforced by men but women also contribute to it. I am sorry to say that women who come into Parliament do not strongly raise issues. The party attitude was evident during the *sati* incident in Deorala as no formal action was taken by the party. All action in terms of meetings and demonstrations was taken by us at an informal level with unofficial members. There was no party line."

"The problem is that women parliamentarians do not work enough to prop other women. It is true that reservation can also lead to any kind of woman coming in but then we have found that the position of women in politics is bad. Women come with connections and use them to move up the political ladder. The 33 per cent reservation was the initiative of Rajiv Gandhi but the Bill had failed in Parliament. In fact the BJP which is today strongly supporting 33 per cent reservation had opposed it then. But today, all parties including the BJP, have changed their position, and everybody has an eye on the women's vote, and the fear that they may be effectively mobilised as in the anti-arrack (country liquor) movement as a vote bank." She feels that 33 per cent reservation for women in *Panchayati Raj* institution has ensured some kind of political participation of women at the grassroots level: "The *Panchayat* elections have brought about a positive change. In fact contrary to popular belief, I have found the literate and semi-educated women are more dedicated and desirous of change. Out of the *Panchayat* system at least 10-13 per cent will rise and provide women candidates for higher levels in the political process."

Najma Heptullah, Speaker of the Rajya Sabha, Congress, belongs to the high-profile political family of Maulana Azad, a well known figure in the Independence Movement of 1947. Although she was not initially involved in politics she was familiar with it, and her leanings were always towards the Congress party. "When I was young my interests were centred around technology and science and I had no inclination towards politics. But many people from my family were active in politics and two of my sisters, in spite of wearing the veil, worked very actively in the women's movement. In my family the emphasis was on education. I was married off into a family which had strong political affiliations with the Congress party of which I also became a member. My husband and I both decided to encourage young scientists and formulated a plan to start a campaign to create a scientific temper at the grassroots level, thereby creating a positive attitude towards such issues as health, family planning, sanitation, etc. I made an elaborate plan and gave it to Mrs Gandhi. She sent me to the Principal Secretary. He in turn told me that I should sell the idea to the politicians. This made me decide that if I wanted to bring about change I would have to join politics and so I joined politics. This was in 1973, and in 1980 I became a member of Parliament."

"Women in politics are important; after all they form 50 per cent of the population. Women had been mobilised earlier by political parties but mainly on emotional issues. Today political parties have been forced to acknowledge the presence of women. Personally, I have never faced any discrimination but I have noticed that the party never speaks for women and whatever they do is mere tokenism. The Panchayat elections have forced political parties to accept women as equal participants in the political system and to accept 33 per cent reservation. Initially even in the Panchayat we saw the wife-sister-daughter (of a male politician) syndrome, but this is bound to change with greater visibility. With more women coming into politics every political party will be forced to accept them and will in fact target them. Indian women have an advantage over the Western societies; we got the right to equality and universal adult franchise in 1947 itself without having to agitate for it."

Mohini Giri, Chairperson of the National Commission for Women (NCW), disagrees with Heptullah's views in that, "the Constitution gives us equal rights but it has not been implemented at all. There are only 36 women in Parliament today. In 1984 I was asked to stand against the BJP, but I found that our democracy is not really ready to accept women as candidates in the elections. Very few Congress party workers were there to help me, no party infrastructure was at my disposal and only my own social workers were there to assist me. I realised that I was in a weak position, and I wondered that if this could happen to me with all my influence, then what happens to ordinary women who have no power?"

Countering claims that women are not suited to politics because they are emotional, she says, "There is nothing wrong with emotions and it is wrong that women are often accused of being emotional. Everything in society is based on emotions and all our decisions are guided by some emotion, so emotion is not negative. Given a chance women can be as rational as men, as rationality is not just a male preserve. Political parties as a whole have not sympathised with women. The mahila (women's) wing of political parties have seldom taken a stand on any issue or followed any concrete direction in their agenda. The other problem is that women who enter politics have to learn on the job. They have no prior training or grooming and this is specially true of the lower-caste women who have come into Parliament. There is a need for concrete training and guidance of women into political participation and the National Commission for Women is formulating a programme for this."

A question that has been repeatedly raised is, why should there be a need for positive discrimination in favour of women after 50 years of independence when our Constitution already provides for political rights for women? The most apparent answer is that laws in statute books are not enough. Political parties must give women the opportunity to exercise these rights. Mohini Giri says that she tried to influence political parties to do this: "When I became the Chairperson of the National Commission for Women, I wrote to all the political parties asking for 50 per cent reservation for women. I attended various women's organisations meetings and made out a list of prospective candidates and sent them to all the political parties. But the results are clear—there are only 36 women in Parliament and 11 States have not sent a single woman to Parliament. So reservation is extremely important and eventually with 33 per cent reservation we may at least get some good women. Moreover, once women are in greater numbers in Parliament they will be able to exert greater pressure and get their voices heard."

"A survey by the NCW of the Panchayat system has revealed that most of the rural women who have been elected are aware of their role, at least 9 out of 10 want to do some work, so the idea of *pradhanpatis* (women as proxies for the exercise of political power by their husbands) is false. We have to realise that initially women are going to face problems but they do want to know about their rights, specially their financial powers. The aim of the NCW is to organise workshops and training programmes to further sensitise these women. Herein also lies the potential for future legislators and parliamentarians. Sensitisation of women at the grassroots level to the needs of health, education, etc. will definitely bring about a change as they will have the power to implement it.

Reservation is just the beginning and the process will take time. We found in our survey that women in Bengal and Maharashtra were far more aware than those in Uttar Pradesh or Madhya Pradesh."[5]

Kumari Selja, Member of Parliament (Congress-I), had not planned a career in politics and says it was a result of circumstances. "I came into politics due to the sudden death of my father. I was asked to contest from his seat in 1988. In my first attempt I lost, but I continued to work with the Mahila Congress for two and a half years. Working with the Mahila Congress was a good experience as it had a properly chalked-out programme that one had to follow and an important part of it was to mobilise women at the grassroots level. Organisations like the Mahila Congress and the National Students Union of India (NSUI) are active and people come to the Congress from these ancillary organisations. I finally won the subsequent election in 1991 and came to Parliament. Because of my father's political standing I did not have to start at the bottom rung of the political ladder. It is true that I entered with certain advantages."

There *is* a certain discriminatory attitude towards women members, Kumari Selja says, "Women are given weak or soft Ministries also because there are so few women who reach Ministerial positions. If more women come in then the situation is bound to change. There is also considerable discrimination at the time of ticket distribution for electoral positions. With reservation I expect the situation to improve. I am an All India Congress Committee (AICC) member, and Ambika Soni is a Joint Secretary, but we do not have a single woman General Secretary. I feel that if we had more women in organisationally important positions, it would greatly improve the situation. It is true that during the independence movement there were a larger number of women involved with the Congress, but over

[5] Our findings in relation to West Bengal and Madhya Pradesh have been similar.

the years their numbers in the political process have declined."

It is very difficult for women to get into politics, says Selja. "Women who join politics do so against odds. I won the 1996 elections against all odds. The fact that I came into politics because of my father no longer matters, as I have proved myself and my connections are now immaterial. When you fight elections you have to always remember that you are dealing with the vast majority of people—both men and women. One cannot just concentrate on women even if we want to, we have to adopt a holistic approach. Elections cannot be won just on raising women's issues. I always give more attention to women-related problems but I have to nurse the constituency as a whole. As a woman I have luckily not faced a situation of harassment by male colleagues but there again my family's political connections have helped."

"Even if we do not fight elections on women's issues we do have women's best interests at heart. At the ticket distribution and selection level, Ambika Soni and I have always fought for women and actually succeeded in getting tickets for them as in the case of Rajasthan in the last election. We fought for a woman candidate and finally managed to give her a ticket in spite of the State leadership's opposition. It so happened that as predicted by us she won. The real problems in tickets come from the State leaderships of the party, and that is where all the discrimination takes place."

She firmly believes that with increasing participation of women, things will change. She cites the example of reservations in Panchayati Raj institutions. "Haryana is not a feudal State like Rajasthan, but it has an extremely rigid caste structure, and the *purdah* system (seclusion of women and compulsory use of the veil) is strong. However, with Panchayat elections things are changing. Initially, women may be controlled by their menfolk but for how long? They are already realising their powers and we are holding training programmes for them. The trend is positive. The Haryana Vikas Party which has won, as they say, with the support of women, has shown no special interest in fielding women candidates, although they did raise the issue of prohibition like all parties. All political parties in Haryana have only one woman MP representing them in Parliament, but with 33 per cent reservation that will have to change. In fact, I feel that they are scared of the Bill being passed, because they do not seem to have any plan of action as to how they will deal with the situation. They have no real base among women, but women activists aspiring to join politics are there and the parties can no longer deny their existence."

The Congress Government in Madhya Pradesh

In order to see the difference between the national postures and policies of the party and its actual State level functioning, we took Madhya Pradesh a Congress ruled State as a case for analysis. Madhya Pradesh has had successive Congress governments with short breaks of BJP rule. A study of the Congress Government, functioning at the State-level in Madhya Pradesh, showed that the party was suffering from a great erosion of its ideological base at the local level which was further compounded by poor organisational infrastructure. Madhya Pradesh is a State which has been under Congress rule for the last four years. It is also the site of many localised movements like the Narmada Bachao Andolan and the movement for compensation of the gas victims of the Bhopal gas tragedy. There are a number of NGOs working in the area of education and adult literacy, but what is surprising is the lack of any movement centred around women's issues. Interviews with various NGOs revealed that women's issues were raised as a part of the larger human rights movement and that there was no real attempt to mobilise women around women's issues. They felt that women's problem did get addressed within organisations like the Gas Pidith Bachao Samiti even as they acknowledged that there was no separate women's movement in Madhya Pradesh. Another fact that emerged was that there was no collaboration between the women's wing of the Congress or BJP with the NGOs. There was no coordination on any women's issue or an attempt to put pressure on the government in relation to women's issues. A Mahila Manch exists but its only function appears to be that of a meeting point for women of different groups, without a specific programme or agenda. The women belonging to NGOs seemed to take pride in the fact that they were not political or affiliated to any political party.

Interviews with various Vidhan Sabha members and women activists also revealed that the Congress was a party ridden with factionalism, with a poor infrastructure and organisation. Women had become the greatest victims in this scenario and the Congress women's wing was a redundant organisation. This became apparent through the interviews of almost all the Congress women. Mrs Hukku, Vice-President of the women's wing, said: "At one time, the party used to support all my efforts but not now. This is primarily because of the factionalism in the Congress. For example, today Pradesh Congress Committee (PCC) chief Mr Bhardwaj and the Chief Minister (CM) Digvijay Singh are at loggerheads. Consequently, I am the sufferer and my work does not get passed in the PCC."

"In Madhya Pradesh, we have tried to work hard but have not succeeded in forming any women's movement. A majority of the communities are uneducated and the women do not move out from the confines of their house. Moreover, there has been no consistent reform movement or social work done for women in Madhya Pradesh. The few women who came to work here were from outside and were transferred after a few years, so the momentum of the work was broken. Even in the Panchayats we find that the women are mostly in *purdah* and do not participate in discussions. The party needs to intervene to sensitise these women through a training programme, but so far no attempt has been made."

"The mahila wing of the State Congress Party has no history of independent action. All directives come from the national party leadership which is the Mahila Congress headed by Girija Vyas. The Mahila Congress in Madhya Pradesh has no proper agenda of its own, no organisational structure and the new members are not given any ideological training. Moreover, the women who come to work for us require some monetary reimbursement for fieldwork expenses. The Mahila Congress does not have funds even for such expenses."

"Personally, I feel that the Congress will not give tickets to women even with 33 per cent reservation, as there are no suitable candidates. Most of the women have done no fieldwork. Further, I have found that women who do achieve power do not support other women or take up the cause of women. Somebody like Jamuna Devi (a Minister in Chief Minister Digvijay Singh's Ministry) may attend a meeting but concrete action on issues raised is limited. It is important to remember that many of them have won because of the caste factor."

Vibha Agarwal, a veteran Congresswoman and Chairwoman of the Commission for Women and Child Development, feels that those who work for the organisation are sidelined while women from outside, wives and sisters of influential persons get the benefits, whether it is a question of party posts or tickets for various political positions. If the efforts made by local women are not recognised they will never be able to rise above a certain level. When these outside women are given tickets, where is the time to establish relationships? Seats will be given to women only when quotas are imposed, but "why 33 per cent—we are 50 per cent of the population, why not 5 0 per cent? Why only in Parliament or Vidhan Sabha —let us start from local organisational bodies, the Pradesh Congress Committee. Some women are coopted into the PCC but these coopted members do not have a right to vote. We have not been able to raise this issue, there are always other more important decisions to be made."

She responded to the question whether women do their job as well as men when placed in a position of political power, by saying "some do, but it will take time and opportunity for women to be equipped with the requisite skills and experience to do a good job. But most of the time they do not get an opportunity to prove themselves. It is often assumed that women from backward communities are uneducated whereas that is not always the case. Even if they are, why is it assumed that they cannot contribute to political life? The only time the party gives any importance to women is at the time of elections. At all other times they are ignored. Very few women are in organisational positions. Good women from good backgrounds do not hold posts. There is a great need to reorganise the Mahila Congress. There are so many women willing to come and work for the Congress but the current PCC leadership does not give them work. If this situation persists these women will go to the BJP because we have not provided them the necessary avenue to give expression to their political aspirations."

Vibha Agarwal felt that there is no questioning of the fact that there are no workshops or seminars to train political activists, "if women are not trained, they are not able to play an active role in political life. For example, in the case of taking up certain projects in one area, grants are given by the center but most women do not know how to get or use it, but if they did it would be to the party's credit. The PCC had failed to provide local women with such opportunities. Effective grassroots level participation cannot take place till such efforts are made."

Manjushri Anand, a member of the Madhya Pradesh Congress Committee felt that there was no women's movement in Madhya Pradesh, and gender consciousness was at its lowest in the political sphere. "In Bhopal recently there was a gruesome incident of a young woman from Andhra who was raped by 50 autorickshaw drivers. In spite of Bhopal being the State capital, there was no reaction by the people. There is very little consciousness about women's rights let alone a women's movement."

"The Mahila Congress has not had elections since its inception. Ram Rani Johar has been its President from the very beginning and she is 70. It is very important for the growth of any organisation that young people join, express their views and there is an interaction between the two generations. More young women should be brought into positions of authority for it is only then that there will be change. The present leadership in the Mahila Congress is incapable of generating any kind of ideology and programmes into the organisation. The Mahila Congress makes no effort to form its own agenda based on local issues and interest. It neither takes up women's issues nor does it provide support to women who work for it."

"The problem with most of the parties is that family affiliations play a very important role in the allotment of tickets. For women like us who actually do all the field work for the party, this is very frustrating. Considering the amount of time and energy we spend, we do not get our due. The Panchayat elections have shown one thing—that there is no dearth of women candidates. We were able to win more than the reserved quota of 30 per cent seats. Women today account for more than 38 per cent of the Panchayat seats. There is no denying the normal teething problems of *Pradhanpatis*, but with the right guidance and training these women will be able to gain full political control. Dismissing women by saying they are not interested is just an excuse. They need to be encouraged and a conducive atmosphere created for them to join politics. It is true that the middle class woman is apolitical and does not want to join politics, but that is not true of the tribal women. Another important point to remember is that few seats are given to women, so in reality the number of women winning is higher than men in proportion to the seats allotted to them."

The argument put forward by Manjushri Anand about the

lack of consciousness or a group identity among the women has also been substantiated by the Geeta Devi incident. Geeta Devi and her husband, Shivendar Bahadur Singh were both Congress members, she a member of the State Assembly and he a member of Parliament. She complained that he repeatedly humiliated her and physically abused her. Many of the Vidhan Sabha members had been a witness to these acts and she asked the Chief Minister Digvijay Singh to intervene to put a stop to the situation. But Shivendar Bahadur Singh, instead of being apprehensive about his actions, after 28 years of marriage allegedly threw Geeta Devi out of the house and there was a stage when she literally had no place to stay. All her jewellery, clothes and valuables have been taken away. She is fighting a case in Court which is yet to be resolved.

Aside from the facts of the case, the way in which the party and the women in the Congress viewed this whole issue is quite significant. The unfortunate part of this whole episode is that most women within the party have viewed this as a domestic quarrel between husband and wife rather than a case of wife abuse and did not feel it important or necessary to stand up for the rights of an abused woman. No help was given to her by the Mahila Congress and she was left to fight her battle on her own. There was a time when it was doubtful whether she would get a ticket to contest in the previous election (Digvijay Singh Government). She was eventually given a ticket once again to contest, but then she was a winning candidate in her constituency. And despite the fact she was the official Congress candidate and her husband a Congress member, he financed a candidate against her. Her official complaint to the party on such a serious charge of anti-party activity went unheard because she was complaining against her husband. He is even said to have put up his own domestic servant against another official Congress candidate who also happens to be a woman and a member of the same family.

Today she is accused of drunken behaviour and

manipulating her husband to suit her ends. The issue today is no longer the fact that she had been beaten and humiliated by her husband but the fact that she was a woman of immoral character who had exposed her personal life to the public. It was an issue she should have resolved within the four walls of her house and she unfortunately brought the matter to the public platform. "Geeta Devi was wrong in making her domestic problems public. One has to protect one's family and keep matters like this private. One has to do it in order to retain one's pride." This statement of Mrs Devendra Kumari, Congress member and former Member of the Legislative Assembly (MLA) clearly reflects the ambiguous attitude of many of the women party members and their lack of concern. The hostility faced by Geeta Devi, even today, has not generated any sense of unity among the women MLAs. The few women in the Opposition who had raised the issue are also, now, quiet in the face of opposition. When we questioned Manjushri Anand, she was defensive, "The problem with the Geeta Devi incident was that she never approached the party organisation for help but met Digvijay Singh personally. Then she took the whole matter into the public arena. She should have approached the party formally. Digvijay Singh is only the leader of the Congress in the Vidhan Sabha not the controlling authority."

The lack of a women's movement was further confirmed by **Kaiser Bia** who runs a school for children and various educational programmes in Bhopal. She had been an active member of the Congress in her younger days and even though she has retired from active politics, she retains her links with the party. According to Kaiser Bia, "women who come into politics, join mainly because of family affiliations or political contacts with various factions of the party. Many of them join with intention of social work and gradually aspire to become candidates without putting in the requisite amount of field work. When I initially joined the Youth Congress during the early seventies there was a definite ideology and direction in the party. Now the situation is different, the party is fragmented, it has no agenda, no target and no work. However, the seeds of this growing lacuna were evident during the 1970s itself. During the seventies in my enthusiasm to work I decided to do a study on the population census of some areas. My work was appreciated by the party leaders but no concrete action was taken to encourage others to do similar work. There was no attempt at further networking or at mass mobilisation."

"This attitude of the party leaders was not because I was a woman but just that they were not interested in work. But at least there was somebody one could approach at that time (the reference is to the Nehru-Gandhi family). Today the situation is dismal as there is nobody left to question the party's action. There is no dissent or questioning within the party of the party leadership. The Congress is still trying to survive on the legacy of the Independence movement."

The experience of **Jamuna Devi**, the Minister for Women and Child Welfare who belongs to a tribal community has been radically different from the upper-caste and upper-class women who predominantly inhabit the political sphere. She initially came into politics as a member of the Socialist Party. Being a village woman she was new to the game. She says, "When I came into politics I had no prior experience except for being involved with the *Adivasi* movement for equal rights. When I stood for elections for the first time in the fifties I was a complete novice and could not even speak. I realised the need to educate myself when I got elected to the Vidhan Sabha. "

Then in the next elections (1957) the Socialist Party changed her constituency and as she did not have a base there, she lost. Her dissatisfaction with the leadership for changing her constituency was evident and she changed her party affiliations. At this point of time the Congress felt that it needed a woman who could work among the tribals, so in 1962 she joined the Congress and fought on a Congress ticket from Dharjau and won, in spite of a small election budget of Rs 5000. She felt that "initially the male politicians were hostile but they never tried to harm me as they try and do now. Due to the liberal socialistic ideology of the national movement I have found that the older leadership used to support women much more than the leaders do now. Once again I contested in 1967 but lost as the constituency was redefined and also I faced opposition within the Congress party. I have learnt from my own efforts and I know that I have survived in politics over such a long period because of my close links with the tribal movement. In 1972, I fought independently as the Congress did not give me a ticket. I was very angry with Mrs Gandhi that she had not recognised my contributions. So I stood as an independent and won. Women have to fight for their own interest. The tragedy is that today the Congress is full of people who are only concerned with their self-interest. Earlier the Congress had some principles, some ideology and a person who was capable got a chance. It had a larger base among the *Adivasis* and *Dalits* which has eroded due to the irresponsible attitude some of the party leaders."

The organisation of the Congress in Madhya Pradesh needs a new infrastructure and a restructuring of its functioning. The present system requires a lot of '*Ji hazoori*' (yes-manship) which she felt she could not do and so she gets into trouble from time to time with the Chief Minister, Digvijay Singh. She feels: "The party does not allow for sharing of power and women are not yet strong enough to fight for their rights. The Congress is still functioning by dynastic rule and this has really disrupted the organisational structure and made the BJP powerful. The problem is compounded by the IAS officers who do not want to work but want to have control over all the available funds. They are not concerned with implementation of schemes. "

"The idea of local governments and Panchayats is good but periodic monitoring of programmes is important as schemes controlled by sarpanchs are not implemented and the villagers are exploited. For example, the *Aganwadi* workers programmes are suffering as the women workers now receive salaries from the *Sarpanches*, who in most cases ask for a commission. The role of NGOs is also dubious in MP as they are often started by wives of bureaucrats and corruption is the norm. Nobody is bothered about the tribal areas, where girls still have to travel 10 kms to attend a school. The only people to have done work in the tribal areas are the missionaries. There is another myth which has been built up that if you are a politician you cannot be honest. Nobody realises that there are some honest politicians and that the amount of money you get does not even cover the expenses of maintaining your office."

Jamuna Devi has been the butt of many a joke. She was laughed at for aspiring to be the Chief Minister or for projecting herself as the leader of the Scheduled Tribes and the bureaucrats were particularly hostile to her. Many attributed easy morals as the reason for her success.

Mabel Robello, a social worker, Secretary, Federation of Madhya Pradesh Women and Child Welfare Agencies—apex body for a number of grassroot level NGOs—felt that the real problem for the non-participation of women was Congress factionalism and women were the worst sufferers of it. She claims that "the government had announced its intention to formulate a State level policy for women and also to constitute State Commission for Women (SCW) and has failed on both counts. Although the Act for the formation of the State-level Commission for Women was passed many years back it is yet to be constituted. I am a member of the government's Committee on Women. This Committee has had only two meetings in the last three years."

"Women in the Panchayats, municipalities and the Vidhan Sabha are fighting a difficult battle and ultimately have to buckle under pressure. For example, Jamuna Devi had a long-standing battle with the Chief Minister but had to finally accept defeat. Women legislators also at times fail to take up the cause of women. A reason for this may be because they have to nurse a constituency and the fear of forthcoming elections is always present."

"My main work is as an NGO but I am also a member of the Pradesh Congress Committee. To be an effective NGO and to assist in welfare programmes, one needs to be on the periphery of political power. There is nothing like a women's movement or NGO networking in Madhya Pradesh and very little tangible work is being done in the area of women's empowerment. Some work is being done in the area of Women and Health by the Holy Cross and by Eklavya in the area of education."

Mabel also felt that in Madhya Pradesh the Mahila Congress is a stagnant, middle class organisation and no concrete work is done at the grassroot level. The Mahila Congress in this State has never agitated for any special women's cause. The lack of any kind of women's movement can also be attributed to the fact that the problems of basic subsistence like *roti, kapda aur makaan* (food, clothing and housing) are so crucial, that the issues of equality and sharing of power do not exist."

Devendra Kumari represents that section of women politicians who have come into power due to their families' political history and feudal power over certain areas. As the wife of the erstwhile Maharaja of Sarguja and an eminent bureaucrat she had a social, economic and political status when she entered politics. She belonged to a family in which her grandfather was affiliated with the freedom movement and was a Congress loyalist. In spite of her husband being a government officer she entered politics in 1971 as there was nobody of the family left to contest from the area. She felt that her position as a Member of the Legislative Assembly (MLA) was better than that of most women because of the recognition and respect her family had in society. "I was tolerated and my views were accommodated far more by the men than in the case of other women. The uneducated women faced a particularly difficult time. Only strong women like Jamuna Devi can survive who, on not being given a ticket by the Congress, fought independently and won. Consequently, the Congress was forced to recognise her. During my tenure as a MLA, I was successful in getting schools opened in my area and also some health services provided. But getting the work done was a difficult task in spite of my contacts with the bureaucracy."

"Due to the reorganisation of the boundaries of my constituency, I lost the subsequent elections. Over the years I have found that the party has deteriorated and only those women who can hang around important leaders survive in politics. The high level of illiteracy also puts many women at a disadvantage and when they come up from the grassroots level they are not taken seriously. In the recent Panchayat election we found that women have come up but they have no knowledge or experience and need to be trained. The party is making no effort to train and bring up the women. The tragedy is that the Mahila Congress is encouraged to speak but its programmes are not taken seriously. In fact, I find that there is no real difference in attitude between the BJP and the Congress. The awareness and enthusiasm found in the Mahila Congress during Rajiv Gandhi's rule has completely diluted today."

The interviews with the Congress party members have clearly revealed that the party provides only a limited space to women and mainly those with political connections. It has become the fertile ground for women of influential political families to join politics. Some of them have managed over time to carve a niche for themselves, but primarily due to their own abilities with little party support. The hostility to women and lack of party support gets further aggravated when a Congress Government functions at a local level. A poor organisational infrastructure and criminalisation of politics discourages women from venturing into politics.

Wherein lies the malaise? Kishore Chandra Deo, Congress Member of the Rajya Sabha, seriously addressed this question.

He did perceive a change in the attitude of the party on the question of women and political participation over the years. "There has been an increasing awareness and concern about women's participation in politics. This consciousness may come from a genuine concern but also from an increasing recognition of women as a possible vote bank. This concern can be seen in the formation of the Mahila Congress in the mid-eighties and the establishment of a Commission on Women. However, it cannot be denied that there was little activism at the grassroots level. I think it is a very important issue, and attempts should be made to encourage women to participate. But the question of quality becomes very important. What kind of political training or organisational training is given to these women to provide the party that quality that you are looking for?"

"It must also be remembered that that there is very little concern for ideology or organisation since the mid-seventies. We do, from time to time, bring out pamphlets and party programmes and manifestos but hardly anyone pays any attention to these because success is not determined by how much you know or how much organisational work you do, and this is true for both men and women. If you presume that men are more aware of the central ideology or concerns of the party you would be mistaken. Much of today's political success depends on latching on to one important political leader or the other. This again makes it difficult for women because it is more difficult for them to cultivate leaders given the traditional and cultural background they come from."

"This was not always the case, as even as late as the early seventies, Congress was still very much a social and economic movement, as can be seen by the package of socio-economic reforms brought forward by Mrs Gandhi after the 1971 elections. All parties in today's political arena are male-dominated parties. But there are a number of lady members who command the respect of their colleagues."

Kishore Deo feels that the declining number of women in politics is due to the criminalisation of politics which makes women most vulnerable. This also raises the question: What kind of men and women get into politics? "Only those women can afford to come into politics who have some political or financial backing from their family. Even for men these family links become very important and is a determining factor in the allocation of tickets. It makes it very difficult for women without political connections to take the risk of sticking their necks out."

"There is no organisational support on the basis of which women can think of entering politics. In the game of politics the party organisation has receded to the background, and powerful individuals started to have the last say. So where was the organisation? Organisational elections have not been held for a long time. Therefore, the party cannot provide the kind of support required. As a result, deserving candidates did not always get the ticket, even in the last election, at least I know about Orissa and Andhra. This is the kind of discrimination that takes place but again this is true for both men and women."

"There is genuine concern within the party to involve more and more women in the political process. There are individuals within the party who may have conservative beliefs about women's political participation but due to the increasing pressure of the women's movement very few will today have the courage to voice these sentiments in public."

The Congress today is organisationally characterised by a culture which is hardly conducive to the participation of women. At the same time its lack of a clear-cut ideological perspective gives it the opportunity of shifting its position *vis-a-vis* women from time to time, depending on which position will give it the optimum electoral advantage. Such decisions may have given it some short-term gains but have ultimately contributed to the marginalisation of women and the loss of people's faith and confidence in the Congress party, specially of the marginalised sections, including women, of its capability to defend their rights and further their interests. By siding with tradition and fundamentalist elements in the context of women's rights, it has inadvertently encouraged communal elements and given their retrograde ideology the much needed acceptability.

Bharatiya Janata Party: Bastion of Tradition

4

The Bharatiya Janata Party (BJP), successor of the Bharatiya Jan Sangh, represents the conservative section in Indian politics. It propounds and extends the ideology of cultural nationalism that emerged during the national movement. It has its base in the two extreme Right-wing organisations: the Vishwa Hindu Parishad (VHP) and the Rashtriya Swayamsewak Sangh (RSS). These constitute what is commonly known as the Sangh Parivar and their combined ideology determines the functioning of the BJP. In fact, almost the entire cadre of the BJP are drawn from these parent organisations and the women's wing is no exception to this rule.

In historical terms, when Lakshmibai Kelkar had approached Hegdewar, the founder of the RSS, in 1936 to admit women into the fold, she was rebuffed. It was much later that Hegdewar actually helped her to form a women's wing, but neither he nor Golwalkar (another eminent leader of the RSS) ever gave importance to the formal organisational status and training of women. The women's organisation within the RSS, the Rashtrasevika Samiti, was initially confined mostly to the RSS strongholds of Maharashtra, Karnataka and Andhra Pradesh. The RSS attitude towards women is best evident in the writings of Golwalkar, who considered the ideal woman to be a mother who helps the cause of the 'nation' by bringing up her children within the RSS framework of *samskaras*—a combination of prescribed family rituals and habits of unquestioning deference to the family and to Sangh values and leaders. His vision of women and the family was imparted in the daily *shakhas* (branch meetings) of the women's wing, and it forms a cornerstone of the ideology of the RSS.

Family and Organisation: The Shakha

The interweaving of the family and the organisation is best seen in the way that the smallest local unit of the RSS, the *shakha* works. The *shakha* enforces patriarchy by the injunction that for all members the authority of the family is indisputable. In fact, even admission to the *shakha* is conditional on this, and the organisation working in close collaboration with the family, seeks to insert itself into the authority structure that rules the lives of women cadres. In other words, the political activism of the women in the Sangh Parivar (known as *rashtrasevikas*) is projected as submission to patriarchal authority, of which the Rashtrasevika Samiti becomes an integral part. Since politicisation occurs as a result of confirmation of familial structures within the Samiti, the wife is firmly told that her role is primarily that of a preserver of family peace, and that the onus of its restoration must lie with her. The Samiti does not approve of divorce and does not provide legal help to those members who may need it urgently. It tries to insulate young members from romantic folly by filling up their daily routine with a heavy schedule of work. The *rashtrasevikas* are encouraged to believe that family considerations should reign supreme in marriage and career choices, and that even organisational work must rely on family sanction.

The business interest of the commercial class also relies on Hindu norms of conjugality. The RSS *sanghchalaks* refer to Sita's chastity and its necessary influence on true Hindu wives. It is only the certainty that Sita's precepts are being followed at home that enables traders to go away on long business trips with an untroubled heart. Such virtue, RSS workers would argue, is in severe contrast to the long inventory of western social and moral flaws that range from widow remarriage, divorce, adultery and drugs to 'sexual orgies' and other depravities. Interestingly, however, social and domestic purity is considered to be actively dependent on a strictly brahmanical self-control over sexuality. The RSS exaltation of the ascetic model (segregation of *shakhas*, celibacy of *sanghchalaks* and of most *pracharaks* and *pracharikas*) marks an important distinction between itself and other similar patterns for youth organisations. The fascists and the Nazi youth fronts had propagated a hard macho attitude and an aggressive male sexuality. Here, however, the ascetic brahmanical model attempts to temper the virility of the male warrior ideal, and contains it within a frame of low-key, monogamous, chaste manhood which carefully regulates its sexual activities for strictly procreative purposes.

The Samiti, through the physical training it gives to its cadres, offers the hope of empowerment to women who face problems of violence and social discrimination within the family. The training creates the illusion of developing women's health and self-confidence; but since the Samiti has no place for minds that seek to explore and question of social exploitation, it forestalls any serious interrogation of patriarchy. Above all, it teaches girls to submit obediently and unquestioningly to decisions regarding marriage, education and choice of career. Thus, parents and in-laws from conservative, upper-caste, professional or trading families find in the *shakhas* an invaluable ally in enforcing familial discipline. The Samiti thus extends its zone of influence beyond the core members into the family and neighbourhood—an extension of its base which is achieved without separate mobilisation.

Even though the institutional link with the RSS was not formally admitted, the *rashtrasevikas* faithfully replicated the training methods and ideology of the Sangh fathers. No attempt was made to move out of the fold of the middle and upper-class confines of the Samiti. As a result, over the years, growth has been limited, especially when compared to the growth of the women organisations of the Left. In spite of being the oldest women's organisation, the strength of the Samiti, according to one *Sanghcalika,* was only one lakh in 1990.[1] But the attempt to mobilise the lower-caste/class women has since been intensified—the BJP has located Scheduled Caste and Scheduled Tribe women as primary targets for the next elections and, for the first time, has formed a new group of full-time women cadres to work for them.

Marginalisation of Women

The Sangh Parivar ideology also makes selective use of the Indian mythological tradition to mobilise opinion in favour of their agenda. The best example of such distortions is the use of mythological figures like Sita and Durga to manipulate women. In the oral tradition, Sita's name always precedes that of Ram, but today *Jai Siya Ram* (praise be to Sita and Ram) has been replaced by *Jai Shri Ram* (praise be to Lord Ram). As Tanika Sarkar rightly points out,[2] Sita, despite her traditionally accepted qualities, seems to have disappeared from the agenda of the BJP, a fate which is tragically similar to that of *Sita ki Rasoi* (the hypothetical kitchen of Sita said to be located near the Babri mosque) that was destroyed by the devotees of Ram during the demolition of the Babri Masjid.[3] With the elevation of Ram to the status of Hinduism's primary god, the pious,

[1] Basu, Tapan, Datta, Pradip, Sarkar, Sumit, Sarkar, Tanika, Sen, Sambuddha, *Khaki Shorts, Saffron Flags,*1993, Orient Longman.

[2] See Basu,Tapan, Datta, Pradip, Sarkar, Sumit, Sarkar, Tanika, Sen, Sambuddha, ibid.

[3] A major political event in history has been the controversy between the Right-wing fundamentalists of both the Muslim and Hindu communities over the Babri Mosque. While the Muslim claimed it was a mosque, the Hindu fundamentalists have claimed it to be the temple where Lord Ram (one of the major reincarnations of God in the Hindu pantheon) was born. The controversy developed into a movement spearheaded by the Sangh Parivar culminating in the mass hysteria of 6 December 1992 when thousands of the Sangh Parivar party workers defied the law and broke the police cordon to demolish the 500 year-old mosque. As the Babri Mosque came crashing down, the voices of many women were heard for the first time. Significant was the communal rhetoric of Sadhvi Rithambara and Uma Bharati.

self-sacrificing Sita no longer has a space in the BJP political agenda. Sita's image next to Ram was believed to preach pacifism—in the *Ramayana*, when Ram goes to destroy the *rakshasas* (demons) for the sages of the *ashram*, Sita enjoins him not to destroy any other creature who is not to blame. Such a consort for a god who, by the Sangh Parivar's definition, is a martial god, is, of course, entirely inappropriate. So Sita must quite naturally be sacrificed, and Durga, portrayed as a martial destroyer of evil, elevated.

Women in Action

The role of the women's wing in the BJP/Sangh Parivar project first became evident in 1992, when a hitherto non-descript and mild organisation acquired a purpose and a role in the cause of the *Hindútva*.[4] The question that must be answered is: Why were so many women so vocal and visible in the course of the most violent phase of the *Hindutva* movement (reassertion of Hindu religious and cultural pride)? The RSS, the parent organisation, is still an all-male organisation and its women's wing, the Rashtrasevika Samiti, has traditionally maintained a low profile. What made a conservative organisation like the RSS change its attitude and give women a defined role? It is important to analyse the position of the Sangh Parivar historically in order to understand its ideology and how this change fits into its scheme of events.

One of the most sinister features of the recent *Hindutva* campaigns has been the prominence given to the militantly communal woman in a variety of unprecedented ways. A

4 *Hindutva* as used by the BJP harps on the common cultural tradition which should be accepted and respected by all. This understanding of Indian culture, as secular groups point out, identifies Indian tradition as the religious and cultural tradition of the dominant community which literally means the Hindus. Thus, denying the plural character of Indian tradition and calling all those subscribing to any other cultural tradition as anti-national.

certain disjunction is noticeable between the continued austerity within the Rashtrasevika Samiti and in the domestic ideology of new *Hindutva*, and the flamboyant militancy of the new woman activist of the Hindu Right. Rural women at Bhagalpur in 1989 as well as upper-middle-class Maruti-driving women at Ahmedabad in 1991 have appropriated active roles at the centre-stage of riot scenes, places where they were hardly sighted before, an ironic inversion of the woman's traditional invisibility.

By the VHP's reckoning, 20,000 *Karsevikas*[5] courted arrest on 4 January 1992 alone at Ayodhya[6] and a total of 50,000 women were involved in the entire December-January round of *satyagrahas* (protest through non-cooperation). It was claimed that these women were so active that, if in popular perception L. K. Advani and his *rath* (chariot) were the visual emblems of *Ram Janmabhoomi*,[7] then the voice and the words that fixed its message were those of women. Similarly, women were present in large numbers at the demolition site of the Babri Masjid, where the women's wing of the VHP dominated. The largest female contingent was from Maharashtra – 12,000. Andhra Pradesh also had a large contingent of 4,000. All the women present were vociferous in their support of the act, even though they did not participate directly in the demolition. They were confident that theirs' was a religious mission and they were willing to give their lives for the cause. It was this sense of a religious mission that legitimised and motivated the change in women's

5 *Karsevika*, a woman who performs *karseva* (service) which means performance of certain duties without expectation of gain as part of her religious and ritual obligation.

6 Ayodhya is a small town in the north Indian State of Uttar Pradesh which is said to be the birth place of Lord Rama, one of the important gods of the Hindus.

7 *Ram janmabhoomi* literally means the birth place of Ram. It was claimed by the BJP and its allies that the mosque was located on the exact site where Lord Rama was supposed to have been born. It was also claimed that there had been a temple located there which had been destroyed by the Muslims and a mosque constructed on its site. So the aim was to liberate the birth place of Ram.

participation from an otherwise passive and supportive role to an actively aggressive one.

The new scenario definitively demolishes a rather comforting article of faith that has prevailed among some feminists: that women are intrinsically a force against communalism, not its active agents, and that they are victims, healers, preservers of community memories during and after riots. Nor can we draw false comfort from the illusion that these women are not speaking their own minds or their own words. While speaking to a group of male *satyagrahis* at Ayodhya, Tanika Sarkar[8] reports that women would often enthusiastically join in when their male counterparts were being interviewed. Chandravati, a woman from Aligarh, excitedly broke into the conversation saying "we have come here to shed blood...., ... the meaning of temple building is that *mullahs* should be hanged, Mulayam and V.P. should be hanged." Vijaya Dube, a would-be *sanyasin* from Ghaziabad, emphasised that with the liberation of *Ram Janmabhoomi,* a whole new world will come into existence. These women were convinced that only when *Hindu Rashtra* is established will the wrongs committed on women cease.

The *Ram Janmabhoomi* movement, then, appears to have effected major breakthroughs in women's political self-activation within the Sangh Parivar, an opportunity that even the earlier communal upsurges had not yielded. Most of these women were from educated middle-class families and professional backgrounds and were regular members of the *Durga Vahini,* which trains them in the martial arts. Ironically, however, the objective of the Parivar in bringing these women to Ayodhya had been to help with the *langars* (community kitchens). The rest of their time was to be spent singing *bhajans* and *kirtans* (devotional songs) and listening to taped inflammatory speeches. The women were also warned to stay

[8] Basu, Tapan, Datta, Pradip, Sarkar, Sumit, Sarkar, Tanika, Sen, Sambuddha, *Khaki Shorts and Saffron Flags,*1993, Orient Longman.

away and not to try and take part in the demolition. Herein lies the contradiction of mobilising women and then fitting them within the traditional mould. In terms of traditional iconography, women are held to be transformed by physical and ideological training into *Durga Vahinis*, reservoirs of violent commitment, but this power is restrained by the same traditional notions of what a woman's societal role is. Through its training of women, the Samiti extends its mythology and reputation into the family and community. Once riots occur, the myths help to strengthen the ideology further and fear and doubt lead to exaggerated notions of Muslim violence. Riots are, therefore, not simply a culmination of *Hindutva* aspirations but are structured into a long-term mobilisation strategy for men and women, as without recurring riots there cannot be an assured and permanent constituency for *Hindutva*. Thus, there is an integral connection between the long-term patient work of the Samiti and the carefully recorded and frenzied shrieks of Sadhvi Rithambara.[9]

The demolition of the Babri Masjid did bring women forward allowing them to play an active role. However, it has to be viewed as just one event and only of limited significance, since the Samiti continues to attach primary importance to enforcing tradition and familial relationships. Very much in the tradition of the national movement, in moments of crisis and at times due to the force of circumstances, women could and did, go beyond their traditional role but only to return to the domestic after the crisis was over, the *Karsevikas* were also activated at the time of the demolition but the perception of their role by the Sangh Parivar did not change. At the Rashtrasevika Samiti office Basu, *et. al* were told quite frankly that the decision to train *Kar Sevikas* was the result of an internal debate that was eventually won by younger Samiti members. Earlier the VHP news-sheets that covered the *shilapujan* and

[9] Basu, Tapan, Datta, Pradip, Sarkar, Sumit, Sarkar, Tanika, Sen, Sambuddha, *Khaki Shorts and Saffron Flags*,1993, Orient Longman.

shilanyas[10] ceremonies of 1989 gave little chance to women to articulate their enthusiasm. Even Rithambara's cassette addressed its invocations to rise and fight exclusively to men: "*Vir bhaiyon jago*!" (Brave brothers awake!).

The post-demolition period shows that the Samiti women have once again gone back to their traditional roles, working within the confines of their family and community in spreading the ideology of the party. Samiti workers concentrate on developing ties with new members, especially with those who have been married into families of the RSS followers. The aim is to expand the RSS network into new kin-groups and new neighbourhoods, rather than into new social groups. The ideology places importance on a person-to-person, inch-by-inch advance that facilitates a totalitarian conquest of a limited area and class. Inspirational feminine examples still relate to motherhood: for example, Bhagat Singh's mother crying after his death, not because she had lost her son, but because she had no other son to be martyred. Even the Rani of Jhansi is invoked as the patriotic mother, fighting to defend her son's rule over the kingdom as he was too young to assert his right. The warrior figure of a queen as a staunch adversary of the British was inserted into the '*Bhaya Prakat Kripala*' video cassette. Thus, even while women like Sadhvi Rithambara and Vijayaraje Scindia were endowed with an exalted position at the climactic phase of the *Ram Janmabhoomi* movement, they are still exceptional, rare figures, and women in general remain a marginal source of mobilisation.

The Sangh Parivar may allow women to join violent movements but they do not encourage them to be involved in village welfare or tribal mobilisation work. Even the *pracharikas*, whole-timers who follow the RSS pattern, remain celibate,

10 *Shilaniyas* means laying of the foundation stone, in this case for the construction of the Ram temple near the mosque. *Shilapujan* meant the ritual worship of the foundation stone before it is laid. Thousands of activists of the Sangh Parivar had gathered for this occasion in 1989.

concentrating on training middle-class women. Their attitude towards caste too is also ambiguous, and they tend to avoid the question. While they proclaim that they do not approve of caste, they do not debate or discuss it on the pretext that it will embarrass the lower-caste members. In fact, they often did not know the number of lower-caste women involved with them on the defence that caste affiliations are not recorded. It is also true that since most of the members are recruited locally from among friends, family members and the neighbourhood, caste conflicts are not an issue for the Samiti.

The young women of the Samiti are carefully insulated from the larger problems that women and dispossessed social groups face. The mode of organisation does not expose *Hindutva* citizens to polluting lower class/caste milieus, as it does not take them away from the domestic environment. It keeps them tied to family interest and ideology, even as it spices up their lives with excitement of a limited nature and reinforces an important public identity. In keeping with the times, the women in the *shakhas* often discuss and give verbal affirmation to modernistic values. For example, the women in the Samiti were quite emphatic that *sati* is an undesirable practice, but they do not feel the need to give expression to their rejection especially in the face of statements made by many of their leaders. Samiti members have so far not taken any noticeable part in women's movements against *sati* or dowry or domestic violence, issues that are familiar to them even in their upwardly-mobile middle-class contexts. Even though they may criticise the practice of dowry, their own families practise it freely. One of the major forms of social work among the Sangh members is to collect dowry items for the poorer members, so obviously the RSS discipline does not ban the custom.

Voices of Protest

In recent years, especially in the post-demolition phase,

there have been some protests by women Members of Parliament (MPs) of the BJP on certain issues, which is a distinct departure from the earlier tradition of the BJP and its parent bodies. This is perhaps in response to the growth of a large modern, educated middle class which forms their major constituency. In its new self-image, the BJP has had to rethink the kind of woman who would provide a representative image of women as the party perceives them. It used a combination of modernity and tradition to construct this image. The confidence of the new educated middle-class had to be reflected and she had to be given a certain space to articulate this new confidence as well as dissent. In order to prevent discontent from sparking any kind of antagonism within the party, the protests are allowed. Moreover, this helps to present an impression of modernity and an image of a progressive organisation that encourages debate, even while allowing for the basic traditional conservative ideology to remain intact. The anger is directed against specific temporary events, for example, the response of some women BJP MPs to the sexist insults heaped on Uma Bharati; the BJP MP and spokesperson Sushma Swaraj being allowed to criticise the Shankaracharya of Puri for preventing women from reading the *Vedas*.

At a seminar on the *Vedas* in Calcutta on 16 January 1994, the Shankaracharya of Puri prevented Dr Arundhati Roy Choudhary, an expert in the scriptures, from reciting the Vedic hymns and ordered her to get off the dais. The Shankaracharya asserted that only men have the right to recite the *Vedas*. The BJP, Congress (I) and the CPI women's wing condemned this action of the Shankaracharya. The BJP spokesperson, Sushma Swaraj, said: "Anything attributed to scriptures or any practice followed, which denigrates the position of Indian women deserves outright rejection ... By virtue of his position, the Shankaracharya should try to eradicate the prevalent discriminatory practices in Hindu society, instead of supporting all such practices which belittle the position of women."[11] The party, she asserted, would oppose all practices which belittle the position of women in the country.

The BJP's categorical stand on the Shankaracharya's remarks came in sharp contrast to its earlier attempts to soft-pedal several hardline statements made by religious leaders during the Ayodhya agitation. At that time, some religious leaders had come out strongly in favour of the caste system, criticised reservations and called for a new Constitution since the present one was "anti-Hindu" according to them. Further, in the past, the BJP had always expressed its deepest veneration for the anti-feminist, anti-Muslim and retrograde casteist rulings of the Puri Shankaracharya (e.g., *vis-a-vis sati*, the building of the Ram temple and the Mandal Report) so its reaction against the Shankaracharya on this issue was surprising. It could be a sign of a new openness in the thinking of the party in the post-Assembly election situation. With the failure of the Ayodhya *mantra* (magical chant) to deliver the goods, the party has been looking around to identify new platforms and issues. This may have made them realise that emancipation of *dalits* and women is crucial to their efforts to expand their social base. It may also be an attempt to change its image from that of an ultra-conservative socially irresponsible party to that of a progressive one keen to keep up with the changing times. Since the beginning of the nineties, the younger generation in the BJP has been modelling the structuring of its auxiliary groups along the lines of women's, and other social organisations, although the core of the party has remained unchanged since Hegdewar's days. As a result, we do see these auxiliary wings surface with reformatory zeal every now and then, but only on relatively minor issues, such as whether women should be allowed to read the *Vedas* as a traditional right.

The protest by its women MPs was acceptable to the BJP

11 *The Telegraph*, 20 January 1994.

also because reading the *Vedas* is a part of traditional Indian culture, to which both men and women should subscribe. The same liberal attitude may not apply when it comes to questioning norms of the family. The BJP ideology has not changed much, despite its new packaging and projection, and that too, only as part of a bid to gain the confidence of the urban pro-change men and women. After the *Rath Yatra*[12] and the demolition of the Babri Masjid, the BJP needed both articulate intellectuals to occupy the middle-class podiums and adroit organisers to fill the stands. The changes within the Parivar provided both, and by allowing dissent on a small-scale among its women cadres it gave them a purpose and place and also prevented them from a demanding a greater role in the actual exercise of political power. However, the essential image of the BJP remains that of a Brahminical party. Uma Bharati's recent protests, and the Gujarat and Rajasthan (in both the States the BJP has seen the emergence of dissident groups within its ranks) crises are all indications of unrest among the BJP cadres, yet whether this unrest is going to lead to an assertion of the women's wing and other groups within the BJP remains to be seen.

The BJP/Sangh Parivar uses movements such as the *Ram Janmabhoomi* to prevent major controversies and suppress agitations from within. The protest allows suppressed hostilities to be directed to outside events without raising consciousness about the oppression of patriarchy or of the family. By protesting against the Shankaracharya's injunction, Sushma Swaraj raised the slogan of equality in the context of religious rites, but this in no way affected the general understanding of

[12] Rath Yatra; the President of the BJP, Lal Krishna Advani, travelled throughout the country in a car constructed like a mythological chariot to garner support for the construction of the Ram temple near the site of the Babri Masjid in Ayodhya. The journey was to end dramatically at Ayodhya. By using mythological parallels or images (the chariot), the BJP leadership was trying to identify with the image of Ram who fought evil and defended all that was good. They tried to construct an image of themselves as defenders of the faith following the same path in today's context.

women and their role in society, the family or the party. When it comes to the issue of actual political participation, women are absent. This was very evident during the Delhi Assembly elections of 1993. Even women candidates were surrounded primarily by men during the campaign. When asked why, one BJP worker said: "We do not like our women to go out." Their work was mainly to convince the women in households to vote for the BJP or to make *parchis* (name and number of BJP voters on the voters' list which enables the voter to vote without having to go through the entire list) but without actually taking part in the election process (candidate selection, campaigning, attending rallies, streetcorner-meetings, etc.).

Change in Strategy and the 1996 Elections

A tactical change in the strategy of the BJP was seen in the 1996 Lok Sabha elections. The Sangh Parivar attempted to tone down the fundamentalist rhetoric of its past and much of the fiery BJP rhetoric that swayed voters during the 1991 elections was missing. The reasons may be many, but the most plausible one is that the BJP was wary of attracting attention as a party that exploits religion for political gains. It could be that it was making an attempt to project itself as a responsible political party in the post-demolition phase. The political fiasco in the Vidhan Sabha election of 1993 in the once-BJP bastions of Uttar Pradesh and Madhya Pradesh, together with its perception of the 1996 elections as the election when it would make a major bid for political power at the Centre, may have also led to a rethinking within the party in terms of the kind of image the party would like to project.

This becomes all the more clear when we compare the party's stand on various women's issues, as the positions and the manner in which it articulated them in the 1996 elections deviate quite sharply from its earlier position on the Roop Kanwar *sati* at Deorala (Rajmata Scindia had openly supported

Sati as part of Indian tradition, today such open support for *sati* would not be articulated even if it was felt). Today, Sushma Swaraj has become the symbol of the independent, working, modern woman, but at heart and in belief a true Indian woman *(bharatiya nari)*. The discourse is cultured, carefully addressed, and naked in its appeal to urban upper-class women who are looking for a woman to represent their interest, without in any way disturbing their existing belief-structures and privileged positions. Cloaked in the fragile garb of a feigned modernity, the soft-spoken *rashtrasevikas* are now in the forefront, and the *Durga Vahinis* (the more militant group) have been forced to fade into the background. It is important to realise the significance and effectiveness of the BJP strategy in targeting women voters. They have been successful in building a unique and dangerous combination of traditional acceptability, with a facade of modern feminist attitudes, and the recipe has met with obvious success. Readings of recent events that insist that the BJP stands for a monolithic militarisation of Hinduism, miss out on the most important characteristic of the post-demolition BJP—its versatility and flexibility in appropriating and moulding modernity to serve its essentially patriarchal and conservative ideology.

> BJP recognises the power of the women's vote. But their commitment to the women's cause ends with this.

In the light of what we have said about the historical evolution of the Sangh Parivar's approach from strong communal rhetoric to milder liberal tones, it is interesting to examine how it projected this in its manifesto for the 1996 parliamentary elections. The manifesto slated 29 points in favour of women. Prominent among them being:

- An end to discrimination against women and an impetus to gender sensitivity.
- Reservation of 33 per cent seats in all elected bodies

including State Assemblies and Parliament.

- Promotion of legal and economic rights for women.
- Uniform Civil Code to ensure property rights and women's rights to guarantee guardianship rights.
- Removal of discriminatory clauses in divorce laws and an end to polygamy; an end to sexual harassment.
- Focus on the non-reproductive health needs of women.
- Support to single and working mothers.
- An end to all kinds of discrimination against the girl child.

These commitments clearly show that the BJP recognises the power of the women's vote. But their commitment to the women's cause ends with this, for they did not field even a single woman candidate in Karnataka, while at the all-India level only 25 women contested under the BJP banner, of whom 14 emerged victorious.

Women Activists of the BJP 5

The ideology that the BJP and its historical forbearers subscribe to provides very little space to women to move away from traditional role definitions. The strong links of cultural nationalism, familial affiliations, and affinity to traditions have all resulted in binding women to an ideology which prevents any real emancipation. An additional limiting factor is that all office-bearers at all levels of the women's wing of the BJP are nominated. The organisation is totally controlled by male leaders, who not only define its agenda but also determine its day-to-day functioning. Since party ideology is the main functioning principle, there is no space for dissent or debates about party policies.

Mridula Sinha is the All India President of the BJP Mahila Morcha and has been involved in the various struggles launched by the leadership on women's issues. She gave us invaluable insights into the organisational structure of the Mahila Morcha and its relationship with the main organisation. "The BJP's Mahila Morcha was started in 1980. This was the period when atrocities on women had increased considerably and the BJP felt that some attempt must be made to cleanse society of these evils. The organisation was started under Vijayraje Scindia and today 75 per cent of the 406 districts have Mahila Morchas. The Mahila Morcha is a nominated organisation and the key posts of the President and Secretary are decided by the party leader; then the party, in consultation with the Morcha President, decides the posts of the State Morcha President and the women to be nominated as heads of various Samitis at the district levels. We have Morchas at the State, district and ward levels and we are now trying to develop

Sabhas at the village level. The Mahila Morcha works directly under the party guidelines. We are an independent organisation but fully subscribe to the BJP ideology and its principles."

"The BJP as a party does not aim only to gain power for power's sake; its aim is to cleanse and serve society. The Mahila Morcha also follows this aim and believes in the upliftment of women. Women have the right to good education, self-respect, dignity and physical security. Our emphasis is on ensuring women their rights but also retaining the family structures, or to at least ensure the survival of the nuclear family. We do not condone any atrocity on women within the family and demand that the legal system take immediate action to give women their freedom. But we would also like to protect our traditions and family. With the declaration of 1994 as the Year of the Family we organised seminars and workshops giving a chance to various generations of women to interact with one another. This will open up dialogue among different generations and prevent the family from breaking up. We feel that the family is the basis of society and at the core of it is the woman. We have to retain the family and also ensure the woman her rights for the better development of society."

"The BJP is the only attractive party for women to join as they get respect and they are not scared. We do face one problem and that is allotment of tickets during elections; at times selecting suitable candidates is not easy. We have fourteen women in Parliament and eight women mayors in the country. The women's wing accounts for 20 per cent of the membership of the BJP. We have to realise that the question of equality is the cause of friction between men and women even within the society. There is no respect for women and in order to ensure it we have to ingrain a sense of respect for the girl child. We cannot just bring in superficial equality , we have to change the position of the woman in the family. The BJP leaders are very sensible and they realise the need to change society. "

"We give ideological training to our women members

through training camps, and seminars. We are also aligned with the Rashtriyasevika Samiti and other Sangh Parivar members. We meet once a year to discuss the plan of action. We are organisationally separate from the RSS and the VHP although we all share the same goals and principles. Our area of work is to spread political education among all sections of Indian women; our area of operation is much wider."

On the question of reservation, Sinha said: "During the Panchayat Raj elections, many women came up and it is a myth that they are being controlled by their menfolk. In reality there has been a change in women. It is true that men will not accept women in positions of authority so easily and time is needed for both to change."

Uma Bharati, BJP Member of Parliament, has played a significant role in the rise of the BJP and was crucial to its image-building during the period of the Ram Janmabhoomi - Babri Masjid controversy. Initiated into the Rashtriya Swayamsewak Sangh at the age of 10 and encouraged by Atal Bihari Vajpayee, eminent BJP leader, Bharati has dedicated her life to the cause of Hindu *dharma* (religion), Hindu culture and society. For her, the fact that the BJP decided to put the temple issue on the back-burner during the elections was a matter of great ideological compromise. Observing that the absence of a Ram wave has engendered disunity in the party, she reiterated that for her, "Ayodhya, Kashi, Mathura are important. Our leaders may change their colour but I will not." Decrying the complacency of the BJP leaders and their eagerness to compromise on various issues, she said that "it would be better to lose the elections than to follow wrong policies."

"We valued honesty and integrity and the leadership is no longer sticking to those ideals. They are under the influence of intrigues and brokers."

"People enjoying the comforts of life, sitting in air-conditioned rooms cannot visualise and understand the agony and hardship of the workers and the public at large. The dedicated cadre is still with the party because of its philosophy. Withdrawing from those lofty ideals and principles, we may be able to win this election, but we will find ourselves nowhere in the next elections."[1]

In an interview to the television news magazine *Aaj-Tak*, she lambasted the BJP leaders for playing on-again, off-again with *Hindutva*, being partisan in ticket distribution, humiliating interlopers from other parties and using and discarding at will sister organisations like the VHP. According to her, by neglecting the aspirations of its backward-caste members, the BJP leadership had contributed to the impression that it was a party for, of and by the upper-castes. This, combined with its increasing opportunism, quick and easy compromises with ideological opponents at the cost of nurturing a loyal cadre was bound to render any immediate victory for the party a short-term proposition. [2]

The fate of Bharati, where even her criticism of the party goes unnoticed, is an inevitable consequence of the BJP's attempts to marry ideology to power. As *The Times of India*[3] analysed:

> Take the two major areas of confrontation in the BJP today—backwards versus forwards and ideology versus growth. She represents a faction of each in both. *Hindutva* may be a magnificent obsession with Bharati, but she is equally a backward caste Lodhi Rajput. This identity, which remained in her subconscious as long as the party shared her zeal for Ayodhya, is seeking an outlet. It is the old Mandir versus Mandal syndrome, really. The stronger the caste consciousness among the BJP's cadres, the greater the chances of their forming pan-political alliances.
>
> The BJP's astute leadership correctly perceives this as a

1 *The Hindustan Times*, 26 April 1996.

2 *Ibid.*

3 *The Times of India*, 4 May 1996.

danger area for the party. The party leadership had gone in a big way for OBC[4] co-option, knowing the BJP's future hinges on Hindu unification. But since their presence in large numbers could breed caste consciousness, it also made sure that the likes of Kalyan Singh and Uma Bharati were in the vanguard of the Ayodhya movement. The strategy worked and the *Hindutva* frenzy effectively suppressed the caste aspirations of the OBCs. And yet, this is where the party think-tank ran into problems. First, the appeasement of the OBCs outraged the party's entrenched upper-caste leadership, especially in a politically volatile State like the UP. Secondly, the party had to retain the affections of its support base, which, as recent surveys establish, is still largely urban, upper middle class and upper-caste. So while Hindu unification demanded that the BJP's leadership gradually move into the hands of the OBCs (the OBCs would be loath to play second fiddle to the BJP in a situation where other caste-specific options are available) this couldn't be achieved without alienating the party's traditional support base.

Uma Bharati's identity is primarily that of a staunch Right-wing believer and a low-caste politician, but not that of a woman in politics. Her recent opposition to the 33 per cent Reservation Bill in Parliament on the grounds that it may interfere with reservation for Scheduled Castes and Scheduled Tribes was strongly resented by all the women in Parliament.

An interview with **Sushma Swaraj** revealed her to be an articulate, efficient politician, a woman who has risen to her position as the spokesperson of the BJP solely on her own merit. It was also evident that she chooses to tread the thin line between modernity and tradition in a quest for a liberal space within the confines of tradition, a space that she may be able to

4 OBC—Other Backward Castes identified by the Mandal Report for the benefit of resevation.

acquire by virtue of her class and political position. Sushma Swaraj started her political career as a member of the RSS and became active in student politics through the ABVP (Akhil Bhartiya Vidyarthi Parishad, the students' wing of the BJP). She feels that her politicisation came with being a part of the ABVP. "Here political training was given on the pattern of the RSS. We followed the inculcation of the RSS ideology of patriotism and nationalism."

Her family was not affiliated to any political party but her husband had a definite commitment towards the Lohia socialists.[5] She joined national politics in the late seventies in support of the Jai Prakash Narayan movement and became a part of the Janata Party coalition in 1977. She continued as a member of the Janata Party in deference to her husband's commitment even when the BJP split and became an independent party in 1980. Finally, she joined the BJP in 1984, "out of disgust when Shahabuddin started the Muslim India campaign in the Janata Party ". She claims that her joining the BJP was acceptable to her husband as for both of them there is a lot of similarity between the Lohia socialists and the BJP. In fact, she feels that at one time both Deen Dayal of the RSS and Dr Lohia were keen to develop a closer bond between the two parties.

If we look at the issues raised in the 1996 election campaign, we clearly see the difference in Sushma Swaraj's campaign from other BJP women's campaigns in the past. She was projected as a woman in control, a modern Indian woman. Middle class, educated and articulate in English, Swaraj is thus virtually the antithesis of Uma Bharati or even Sadhvi Rithambara, and this difference was reflected in her campaign as well. While the two latter women had campaigned solely on the basis of their ideological commitment to *Hindutva,* making no reference to their gender, Swaraj in fact made efficient use of gender stereotypes. For example, she felt that her real

[5] The Socialist movement in India was fragmented into many groups.

advantage in the polls was being a woman, according to her as women have more patience, do not get provoked and cannot be corrupted. Although a believer in social justice for women, she cautioned that women's empowerment must take place in keeping with 'Indian traditions'.

Indian tradition and culture was, in fact, a major plank in Swaraj's campaign, but at least superficially unlike the *Hindutva* approach to Indianness, the emphasis here was on Indian family traditions and morality, rather than the exclusionist view propagated by Bharati. For example, Swaraj argued that the spread of AIDS in India is the result of Indians turning their back on our glorious heritage. Consequently, it is necessary for Indians to go back to our traditional culture and make morality a part of the school curriculum, besides increasing the vigilance over the blood banks and increasing central outlays on health. On the other hand, the introduction of sex education in schools also presents a threat to our culture, as sex-education teaches children the use of condoms which in itself is an invitation to indulge in sex.

On other social problems like poverty and social justice for women, Swaraj observed that child labour, population and malnutrition are inter-related problems and each perpetuates the other, with poverty being the main cause. Claiming that poverty is due to over-population, Swaraj declared that the BJP will use the carrot-and-stick method to check population, debarring those who have more than two children from contesting elections and giving cash incentives for having female children. An interesting point that emerges is that the sections of society which this kind of argument will exclude are precisely the poor and backward section who tend to have large families. Detailing her accomplishments as a woman leader, Swaraj said that she had worked hard for the education of girls as the Education Minister of Haryana. Speaking about the efforts of her party for broad-based participation of women, she said: "We have already ensured greater participation of women in politics and other inter-related institutions by fixing quotas for women in elective offices at various levels," as this will result in greater awakening among women.[6]

During the campaign for the 1996 elections she acquired tremendous popularity among the people of South Delhi because of her open and accessible manner. Her campaigning was door-to-door and she consciously appealed to women, asserting the importance of women's rights, but within the traditional norms. Herein lay her appeal as far as the moralistic middle class is concerned. Women were to have rights and freedom but within a strictly defined role. Sushma Swaraj was declared elected with a record margin of 1,14,472 votes.

After the parliamentary elections (1996) in which no party succeeded in getting a clear majority, the leader of the single largest platform, Atal Bihari Vajpayee of the BJP, was invited to form the government. Sushma Swaraj, was included in his Cabinet. An analysis of her speeches and the views expressed by her during her brief tenure of three weeks clearly reflects the BJP's attitude towards women and their role in society. She made it clear that she was in favour of a media that stood against corruption and was free from vulgarity. This brought into focus the BJP's stand on the issue of censorship of the media. According to Sushma Swaraj, the growing vulgarity in television programmes had rendered them unfit for "family viewing" which had made the factor of "parental censorship" almost ineffective.[7]

Swaraj's quoted remarks that female news-readers on Doordarshan wear "semi-transparent clothes" and need to dress much more circumspectly, stand at variance with her professed support for media autonomy. Apart from being factually off-the-mark, the last thing Doordarshan's news-readers can be accused of is showing too much flesh—the Minister's views betray a certain anxiety that is far from

6 *The Hindustan Times*, 25 April 1996.

7 *The Times of India*, 31 May 1996.

reassuring. While many people may share the view that television is getting too steamy, few will be comfortable with Swaraj playing the role of moral guardian. Throughout the world, societies are confronting the dilemma of how to maintain their own cultural moorings in a situation where outside influences are increasingly difficult to block out. Virtually nowhere has this been achieved democratically, but apart from the dangers inherent in allowing the state to dictate what should be the representation of women, there is the added factor in our country of the great cultural diversity which makes any uniform formulation socially oppressive.

Sushma Swaraj generated considerable debate when she banned a Videocon commercial from Doordarshan. Swaraj's line of argument needs to be viewed with grave misgivings. The Videocon commercial showed a woman being ushered inside a house by her husband to see the new television set he has bought. Seeing the television, her face lights up, she smiles. Sound burst forth from the TV in a gush of air that portrays the force of the sound system. As a result the long dress the woman is wearing lifts, and she presses it down. Her husband and she do an impromptu twirl on the floor and the commercial ends. Swaraj found this commercial so offensive that she decided it must be banished forthwith. The question here was not even of depicting woman as a sex object because surely a dress that lifts momentarily, showing very little of the woman's anatomy is hardly so objectionable as to be taken off the air. Perhaps the objection was that she was wearing a skirt and not a *sari*. On being questioned on the controversy, Swaraj said: "I never talked about dress code for news-readers. I was asked about parental censorship—I said that Doordarshan must give better programmes than others. Only then will parental censorship have any meaning. Doordarshan should not ape the Western media and forget our traditions. I personally believe that one cannot enforce a strict dress code in the media but I will not allow nudity on the screen. A woman has the space to decide what she wears, but when she comes on TV she is in public space. She has to adopt a code of conduct. In her personal life, a woman can wear or not wear anything it is her husband's wish. If a tribal woman wants to visit the market bare-chested then she can; that is, if her husband does not object. But if she comes on TV she has to subscribe to a dress code."

Swaraj also claimed that such commercials are against Indian culture. What of Indian women in Goa and urban cities, who wear skirts as a matter of course? What our native brand of cultural homogenisers fail to realise is that India is a culturally diverse country. We have cultures that vary greatly in terms of dress codes, of what constitutes the appropriateness of how and what to wear. The backless *choli* (blouse) worn by many rural women or the humble *langoti* (loin-cloth) preferred by tillers of the soil, though they expose much more of the human anatomy, are as Indian as the *sari* or *chador*. Do we exclude all communities and cultures from access to the media because they do not fall into the middle-class perception of what is appropriate? We must therefore resist the temptation of converting the diverse cultures and tradition of India into a synthetic, standardised product to be imposed on one and all.[8]

It is also important to remember that where the crux of the fundamentalist rhetoric is a call for a return to culture and tradition, it is almost always a call addressed to women. When Western dress is rejected, no one demands that men stop wearing suits and ties. It is the woman who has to conform to the traditional dress. The tool of cultural nationalism enslaves women to be the perpetuators, custodians and practitioners of their own oppression. The entire argument put forward by Swaraj reflects an urban brahminical ideology that views women as the repository of morality and traditions, and gives her the right to determine the way in which other cultures occupy the public media space.

Swaraj has also expressed unhappiness over Doordarshan

8 *The Times of India*, 21 May 1996.

showing clips on AIDS prevention and family planning during prime time, because the viewership during prime time consists of children too. She is known for her antipathy to sex education in schools and she banned a programme *'Karan Vaali Baatein'* on FM Radio, because, according to her, in the garb of sex education and AIDS awareness, such programmes promote 'adultery'. Perhaps Swaraj would prefer children to grow up either ignorant of the basic facts of life or with warped ideas and incorrect information? Swaraj also talks of the 'threat' posed by foreign satellite channels. Even the most cursory media watchers could tell her that it has been proved beyond any doubt that an abysmally small number of people watch these foreign channels. Indian programmes, in their own languages, are far more popular. The big success stories in television today are not Star Plus or Star Movies but channels like Zee TV and Sun TV. What was commendable about Swaraj was that, in spite of the insecurity of her tenure she immediately sought to address the problems in her Ministry (Information and Broadcasting). She planned a three-week work agenda which included rethinking on uplinking facilities, putting an end to cultural pollution and setting into motion the process of granting autonomy to Doordarshan and All India Radio.

On the question of the attitude that male colleagues had towards women in her party, Swaraj is quite categorical: "We have to accept one fact, that our society is male dominated, parties are male-dominated and women often get treated as decorative objects. However, I disagree with the image of the BJP as an anti-women party. As a woman I have not faced any discrimination in the party—I have had the opportunity to be the National Secretary in 1984, and was involved in the decision-making processes. At present I am the spokesperson of the BJP. In fact the BJP has formed Samitis at the grassroot level and each Samiti has to have two women. We do not recognise a Samiti if two women are not a part of it." Sushma Swaraj also asserted that the women's wing of the BJP was active and would soon holding meetings to adopt a common agenda to oppose the "satellite invasion of the foreign media which is corrupting our tradition and culture".

"We have 14 women in our National Central Committee, women are working in Sena Samitis. All women members of the Sangh Parivar are to meet sometime this year (1996), where the women will convey their feelings and their problems. There are 22 such organisations, which will meet."

On the issue of reservation for women, Swaraj is equally vehement: "Reservation of 33 per cent will make a great deal of difference in a house of 544. Many men say that women are silent, the question is how many men out of the 544 actually speak? Why do people say that women in Panchayats have not spoken? One should not forget the scale and history of social oppression women face. Wnen women come into Panchayats they will make a difference, as their agenda is different. They will look at issues of health, water and sanitation which affect their immediate existence and are very real issues. Now also women are emerging in the campaigns and there has been an increase in Mahila Morchas. The resistance of women to politics is due to mafia and big money, but reservation may be able to overcome these limitations and will result in greater participation of women. I do, however, feel that women themselves must make the effort and they have to be meritorious."

Thus it is evident that the BJP today is a party in crisis, having lost the zeal and fervour of the pre-demolition period. It is a party which is consciously trying to change its image of an anti-woman party with the presence of women like Sushma Swaraj. Its image-building has succeeded to some extent at the national level but at the State level the situation is far more complex. The issues confronting the party, in a State like Rajasthan for instance, a society whose very essence is based on a feudal structure which oppresses women, are far more difficult to resolve. In such a situation, in the face of political interest, the facade of liberalism has collapsed.

Rajasthan: An Unending Struggle

In Rajasthan, the BJP State Government is led by the charismatic Chief Minister, Bhairon Singh Shekhawat, whose control over the party is absolute (we can even go so far as to say that the BJP wins on his strength) and who belongs to the relatively liberal, non-RSS section of the party. However, as far as women are concerned, this liberalism is just a facade and there are many women like Ujwala Arora in the party who have won Assembly elections time after time (seven) but have never been given a ministerial post. Political advantage rather then fairness determines the allocation of berths. The two women Ministers in Bhairon Singh Shekhawat's government are independent candidates who had been denied a party ticket at the time of elections. Both of them—Shashi Dutta and Narendra Kanwar—have been said to have agreed to offer their support to the government on the condition of being given a ministerial birth. Moreover, the social structure is still very feudal and most of the Ministers belong to the upper-castes. Most Vidhan Sabha members said that caste played a very important role in ticket allotment, with Rajputs playing the dominant role. All good posts in government are assigned to Rajputs and according to their own perception the lower-castes are discriminated against.

Renuka Panicha, a university teacher by profession, and an activist in the NGO women's movement, points out that, in Rajasthan women have no say in society even today, especially at the grassroots level. Men determine everything and the pressure on any woman who tries to assert herself is tremendous. In Panchayats, where the NGOs are active, they are able to encourage women to play an active and productive part, but such intervention is not possible everywhere. Educational levels are still very low among women, especially in the tribal areas. Middle-class women hardly report atrocities and there is no attempt among certain communities (Rajputs and Muslims) to initiate any kind of social reform to improve the status of women within their communities.

Rajasthan continues to be a stronghold of old feudal values, a State in which there has been very little attempt to break the oppression of social structures *via* reform movements and the like. Child marriage and female infanticide are some of the most oppressive social customs still practised. Early child marriage not only means bondage for girls but also leads to the poor being indebted to the feudal lord of the area. These customs are reinforced by the lower-castes in order to acquire social status and acceptability within society. In fact any attempt to defy the feudal order or existing traditional customs is often suppressed with violence. Incidents like the *sati* in Deorala in 1987 and the Bhanwari Devi case more recently, are not isolated, and both events have had wide implications for the political scenario. On the one hand, while issues such as these have consolidated the women's movement in the State, on the other, they have forced political parties to address women's issues.

The first signs of a desire for change emerged during the anti-*sati* agitation. As Renuka Panicha said: " I was associated with the anti-*sati* movement and filed a writ petition in the High Court in order to obtain a stay order against the *chunri mahotsav* (ceremony on the tenth day of the *sati*).[9] There was no political party involved with us except the AIDWA. No Vidhan Sabha member from the Congress Government was ready to speak out and the emerging BJP had decided to support the pro-*sati* Dharma Raksha Samiti."

On 4 September 1987, Roop Kanwar, a young Rajput woman was burnt to death on the funeral pyre of her husband. She was an 18 year old, educated girl and had been married for only six months. Her marital life was known to be disturbed

9 After a certain period of mourning a particular kind of *sari* (chunri) which is worn by brides at the time of their marriage is brought by the girl's relatives, to immortalise the fact that such women can never lose their husbands.

as her husband was suffering from a mental disorder. On her husband's death, when her *sati* was announced, her parents and family were not informed. Reports indicate that the local authorities were aware of the planned *sati* but very little attempt was made to stop the event. The incident sent shock-waves throughout the country leading to strong protests by women's organisations, especially the AIDWA. The Congress (I) Government in power failed to make any attempt to stop the glorification of *sati*. In spite of a High Court order banning the *Chunri Mahotsav*, three lakh people visited the *sati sthal* (the place of *sati*) in Deorala to attend the *chunri* ceremony. The site became a popular pilgrimage spot and Roop Kanwar acquired the status of a *Sati Mata* to be worshipped, in keeping with the traditions of Rajasthan, where till today many old *sati* temples run schools preaching the glorious traditions of *sati* to young girls. The creation of a pilgrimage spot is of course also profitable business for the controlling family.

The issue gradually acquired larger political dimensions when the newly formed Dharma Raksha Samiti (DRS) consisting of all those who supported *sati* in the name of religion, took on itself the responsibility of preserving Hindu religious freedom. The women's wing of the Congress (I) protested against the *sati* incident but very little pressure was put on the Congress (I) Government to take action. The State Government made some feeble attempts to stop people going to Deorala but the prayers at the *sthal* continued uninterrupted. Roop Kanwar's in-laws were arrested but were released soon after. The central Congress(I) Government remained silent until December 1987 when it finally came up with the Anti-*Sati* Act and that too due to outside pressure. The Act, however, was riddled with problems as it made the woman an equal abettor in the crime, to be prosecuted as an attempt at suicide if she survived.

Women's organisations under the leadership of the AIDWA, organised a large protest march. A major campaign issue was that *sati* can never be voluntary as it is committed due to the physical or psychological pressures women are subjected to in society. The life of a widow is so deprived that at times death seems a better option. They demanded that stringent laws should be enacted to ban not only *sati* but also ban its glorification. Any person who watches a *sati* taking place should be considered an abettor in the criminal act. The protest of women's organisations eventually led to the resignation of the Harideo Joshi's Congress (I) Government and attempts to contain the glorification of *sati* at various Rani Sati temples. The battle was thus partially won by the women's organisations. But a recent court judgement (1996) released all those arrested for abetting and forcing Roop Kanwar to commit *sati*. This clearly shows that legislation is not enough to change people's perceptions and attitudes regarding a practice as gruesome as *sati*. The BJP was the main opposition party, it did not actively protest against this gruesome act; on the other hand, some of its leaders openly supported it and even visited the site.

The situation repeated itself in the Bhanwari Devi case, with all remaining silent again, except for the AIDWA which is actively involved in the campaign. Bhanwari, a poor village woman became part of the Rajasthan Government's Women's Development Programme, working as a *saathin* (a community worker) for social change in the areas of health and upliftment of women.[10] Her commitment to the State Government's drive to put an end to the social evil of child marriage resulted in her being gang-raped in the presence of her husband. She filed a complaint and finally after a year her case was heard. A Central

[10] Bhanwari Devi became a *saathin* in 1991 and started visiting women and collecting them around issues which effected their lives. In spite of considerable opposition from the men of the area she managed to create an active group in her Bhateri village. In 1992, the Rajasthan Government passed an order that child marriage should be banned and that no marriage should be allowed during the period of *Akha Teej* (in May when in one night hundreds of children are married). The two weeks before *Akha Teej* were to be observed as anti-child marriage fortnight. Like all *saathins* Bhanwari Devi took up the task of preventing all such marriages in her village by trying to convince the women.

Bureau of Investigation (CBI) enquiry was launched and two of the accused, Gyarse and Badri Gujjar, were arrested. The Jaipur High Court also castigated the authorities for delayed action and for allowing the culprits to flee. The subsequent legal battle and the eventual acquittal of the five prime accused in the case has raised many legal, political and social questions about the status of women in India. The incident is very important because it brought various NGOs and political women's organisations together in unified action. The struggle has not ended and it is evident that pressure for change can be exerted if adequate participation of women is generated.

On 15 November 1995, the Sessions and District Court (rural) at Jaipur acquitted the five accused men against the charge of rape but held them guilty for conspiring and beating Mohan, Bhanwari's husband and manhandling Bhanwari. Under the judgement they were sentenced to six months plus three months of simple imprisonment. The order was to be enforced after a month, giving them time to appeal to the High Court. By then Gyarse and Badri had already spent two years

One such marriage was to take place in her own house (husband's brother). Her attempts to stop the marriage failed due to social pressure and she complained to the police. On 5 May 1992 the police came into Bhateri and stopped all marriages and this soured Bhanwari's relations with her in-laws and members of the Gujjar community. The repercussion of her actions proved to be severe. She was treated like an outcaste and expelled from the *Kumhar Jat Panchayat.* However, matters did not end here. On 22 September 1992, Bhanwari in the presence of her husband was gang-raped by 5 men identified as Badri Gujjar, Gyarse Gujjar, Ramsukh Gujjar, Ram Karan Gujjar and Shravan Pandey. Her husband was beaten and held while two of the men raped Bhanwari.

The struggle was endless and a medical examination was only conducted after 52 hours when evidence was destroyed. Finally due to the pressure of the Mahila Vikas Project the FIR was lodged but the police held back investigation. In spite of repeated appeals and verifications of Bhanwari's statement they continued to doubt her story. The women's organisations in Jaipur put considerable pressure on the State Government and rallies in support of Bhanwari were organised and the matter was taken up in the media. The State Government authorities instead of meeting the women decided to use force to disperse them but finally the State Government had to concede. The case was transferred to CBI in Delhi. However, the situation was no better as the CBI harried Bhanwari to make her statement 9 times and it was due to the intervention of women's in jail and were exempt from the punishment. The other three out on bail were to carry out the punishment. The decision of the judge seemed to have ignored the testimony of Mohan and the judgement discredits his testimony by stating "in our society how can an Indian husband whose role is to protect his wife stand by and watch her being raped?" Bhanwari's own testimony as a witness was completely trivialised and the 52-hour delay in medical examination was ignored. The judge also went on to say the accused were respectable middle-aged men while rape is usually committed by teenagers, and that since the men were upper-caste including a Brahmin, the rape could not have taken place as Bhanwari was a lower-caste woman. The judgement has been condemned by many women's groups who are supporting Bhanwari in filing a case in the High Court. The protest against what happened to Bhanwari was primarily from NGOs and AIDWA. Protests by the Congress MPs has been insignificant and the BJP, which is the party in power, is silent.

However, a certain caste group within the BJP whose members were involved in the incident, actively attacked women's organisations for their support to Bhanwari. On 15

organisations, of Delhi and Jaipur that Bhanwari and her husband's statement was recorded by a Magistrate under Sec 164 and finally it became the basis to chargesheet the accused after one full year. In all this Bhanwari went through acute mental crisis and was compensated with Rs 10,000 only from the Prime Minister's Relief Fund. Following the chargesheet in September 1993 the police arrested the five accused, seventeen months after the crime was committed. In April 1994, the High Court granted bail to the three co-accused who had helped the two main accused to perform the act of rape. In November 1995 the District and Sessions Court acquitted all the 5 accused. During this entire battle Bhanwari was pressurised to withdraw the court case. In February 1995 over 30 newly elected Panchayat Raj representatives of Bhanwari's area, under the active leadership of the local BJP MLA, attacked Bhanwari and her *saathin* colleagues. They insisted that she withdraw the case and they called for a boycott of the WDP. This open abuse of power was condemned by the women's groups. The National Commission for Women asked the Rajasthan Government to conduct an enquiry which is still in process.

The trial in court started in October 1994, and in the process five judges were changed so the judge who finally delivered the judgement was not the one who heard Bhanwari's

December 1995 Panicha recalled, "We took out a rally against the growing atrocities on women. In reaction the local BJP Member of the Legislative Assembly rounded up BJP women and took out an anti-Bhanwari rally. The tone of the entire rally was vicious and directed against so-called home-breakers and feminists. We met the Chief Minister and Sushma Swaraj to register our protest but no action has been taken. The net result of the entire agitation has only resulted in the government clamping down on the Women's Development Programme (WDP), and scrapping of the *saathin* programme."

Renuka Paniche felt that "the government does not want to take responsibility for the hostile conditions in which these women work and thus have to provide protection. The hostility faced by women at the grassroot level restricts the growth of any movement. In Rajasthan sex violence is not even considered an issue, consequently political parties do not respond to it. We are fighting a battle with our backs to the wall as women have no say in society and men determine everything."

Extremely disheartened by the lack of political will on the part of the major parties to withstand feudal and patriarchal pressure, Paniche observes that "the main problem is that political parties have no consistency in their approach to women. In fact that is why I decided not to join a political party. One gets bound by party ideology and there is no democratic thinking. In the case of the Congress, Dr Girija Vyas has made some statement in support of the Bhanwari issue but the Mahila Congress at the level of the State is weak and ineffectual. Left Parties always support the NGO movement and AIDWA is always with us in the case of women's issues. In the Municipal Corporation there were 23 women of the BJP and we tried to mobilise them but in the Bhanwari Devi case we received only

and Mohan's statement. The bias and insensitivity of the judicial system in dealing with cases of rape are evident in the fact that Bhanwari's statements in court were recorded in camera in the presence of seventeen people. This included the judge, clerk, reader, five accused, two lawyers and 7 lawyers for the accused. She was made to describe the whole crime in detail and was cross-examined on it.

a hostile reaction. Some Vidhan Sabha members do assert that the CM is a progressive man, in actuality he is as conservative as everyone else in his party. He rules his party with an iron hand and as far as women are concerned, the party attitude stems from his approach to the question of women's issues."

Kavita Srivastav, Coordinator of the United Front of NGOs[11] said: "The political parties have not taken any action in the Bhanwari Devi case. There have been individual instances of protest like Girija Vyas, who was charged with contempt of court when she publicly protested against the court judgement. She had to finally withdraw her statement and apologise. Beena Kak of the Congress also faced a considerable amount of flak when she openly supported us because the Congress is scared of losing the Gujjar vote bank." Srivastav also asserts that, except for AIDWA, women's wings of political parties like the BJP and Congress do not play any role in most progressive movements. In contrast AIDWA had played a very positive role and had actively participated in the NGO networking and formed an effective pressure group. The surprising fact is that the Left has no substantial presence in Rajasthan but its mass organisation AIDWA has shown a strong presence among the women's organisations. Most of all, it has managed to establish a credibility of its own.

Srivastav also reported another recent incident of atrocity that has cast further doubt on the BJP's pro-woman assertions: "Rachana Gupta a young girl was employed with the Navyog Vikas Samiti run by a BJP activist Shalini Sharma. She was drugged and blackmailed into sexual exploitation. Finally she escaped and complained to a women's organisation in Alwar and an FIR was lodged. The Congress party, for a change, did support us and raised the issue in Parliament. The BJP Government is not ready to take concrete action on the issue.

[11] Almost all NGOs involved with the concerns of women are coordinating their effort to get justice for cases like that of Bhanwari Devi, and have formed a common front known as the United Front of NGOs.

Shalini Sharma and her husband are in hiding and the police is making no attempt to find them and arrest them. In fact BJP party workers are trying to portray Shalini Sharma as a woman who is being victimised for her success as others were jealous."

Srilatha is a member of a Marxist-Leninist group, and works as an activist among peasants and in trade unions. She points out the weakness of the Women's Development Project (WDP) as well as the NGO movement. According to her, the WDP (begun around 1984-85) was a World Bank project and was forced on the people from the top, with no support at the grassroots level. The *saathins* were employed by the government and consequently a *saathin* trade union was not allowed. Even the NGOs, in their own interest, did not support a unionisation of the *saathins*, leaving them almost defenceless without united organisational support. She says, "In fact, the problem with the women's organisations here is that they do not have a concrete ideology. They just try and mobilise along a particular issue. They are all foreign-funded organisations and the dangerous part is that they are not accountable to anybody except their funding agency. In this respect, political parties are far more accountable, they at least have to face the electorate every five years."

"Politics is the ultimate wielding of power as it empowers the individual to control the forces of production and distribution of wealth. The problem is that intellectual women do not want to fight for their power, they want it to be given to them which is not possible. Women in the upper-classes have never had to fight for their economic and academic equality, but political equality cannot be acquired without fighting. Women who are not facing the conflict of patriarchal structures are the rich upper class women who are educated. They have the money to employ servants and do not have to face a hostile situation at home. They are not bogged down by domestic work. As far as the BJP is concerned if there had been no reservation in the Panchayat and tribal areas they would not have put up a single candidate. Over the years I have found that all parties have adopted a negative attitude towards women, and with Shekhawat there has been a further resurgence of conservative norms. Women chosen for the Panchayat elections by the BJP are women who can be coopted into the system and can be corrupted. They are as feudal in their outlook and move along acceptable norms. The tragedy is that no political party or NGO has today taken up the training of women."

Srilatha's party (CPI-ML) has taken up training programmes for women. "In order to survive in politics women have to be more aggressive. I have been accepted as a leader in the Kisan Sangathan and I have forced some decisions on the farmers. They have come to accept the idea of joint *patta* (land ownership deed) with their wives. They have also decided they would take joint action in case of atrocities on women, especially issues such as wife beating and alcoholism. Personally I feel that male education is important because all parties suffer from the same patriarchal norms. At times women find it easier to manipulate these structures and enter politics with the help of men and consequently become oppressed by them."

The picture for women under the BJP Government is dismal. Women face the dual oppression of caste and gender, and women party members fail to see the discrimination and often help to reinforce the conservative ideology of the party. **Ujwala Arora** is a strong RSS supporter. She has been an MLA seven times. She felt that the whole case of Bhanwari was false and that it was a means by which women sought to trap men. "Since I belong to the area I had the whole case investigated and found that Bhanwari's statement was false." She is convinced that Bhanwari had fabricated the whole issue and condemned her for what she called Bhanwari's craving for publicity. No woman, according to her, who has been raped would expose herself and her family to such publicity. "I even had the Shalini Sharma case (refered to earlier by Kavita Srivastav) investigated and it appears that it is a personal fight.

I have hauled up the party on women's issues as in the Kanta Khemkar case in 1983 when I found her in-laws guilty of burning and killing her. But every issue must be investigated and men should have an equal right to speak, not just women. My party is very supportive to the *mahila* wing and when we approach the leaders with a concrete programme they do consider it."

The independent candidates (who were both inducted into Chief Minister, Bhairon Singh Shekhawat's Ministry) Shashi Dutta and Narendar Kawar were much more sympathetic to the issue and felt that Bhanwari Devi must be given relief. **Shashi Dutta** said: "I have found that often issues related to women are treated frivolously in the Vidhan Sabha. I have strongly asserted that the Bhanwari Devi case should be looked into and the poor woman must be given relief. The issue is not just a party issue but a social issue. Even in the Shalini Sharma case I felt that a proper investigation must be done and the party should take responsibility for arresting the culprits. But we must realise that women in the Vidhan Sabha rarely have the opportunity to speak and when they do speak they are heckled. So it is very difficult for a small number of women to assert themselves on any issue in the Vidhan Sabha. This is very similar to the situation which women face in courts and with the police. There is a drastic need to change the legal and political system so as to make it gender-friendly. The tragedy is that in the last five decades the situation has not changed and so the legislature has also remained the same. When a woman is raped or beaten the issue is no longer a private issue. It is a public matter and needs to be investigated."

Personally she feels it is very difficult for women to enter politics. "Women in politics are generally treated with suspicion and therefore a woman has to be strong enough to take on the dual responsibility of managing the home and her public life. An uneducated woman often finds herself in a difficult situation. Political parties tend to give tickets to educated women who belong to *Raj Gharanas* (royal families) and have never really stepped out of the domestic sphere. Many a time women who have recently lost their husbands are given seats in order to create a sympathy wave. The problem essentially starts with our social system in which we have to always identify ourselves in relation to husbands or fathers and a woman's individual identity is not recognised."

Belonging to a scheduled caste or backward caste apparently made matters worse. Even within government, women and other weaker sections face hostility when they raise any question about the unfairness with which they are treated. The incident of **Shashi Dutta** joining other scheduled caste MLAs in submitting a memorandum to the Chief Minister is very revealing. It shows how upper-caste dominance works in a feudal state like Rajasthan and how dissent is dealt with within the government not just the organisation. Thirty-two Scheduled Caste MLAs signed a memorandum demanding equality of treatment in government; it was claimed that Shashi Dutta had not only signed the memorandum but also mobilised Scheduled Caste MLAs and emerged as their leader. As there are almost forty Scheduled Caste legislators in the Assembly and the BJP Government does not enjoy absolute majority, it became a matter of grave concern and a question of survival for Bhairon Singh to scuttle any such discontent. Consequently, Shashi Dutta had to face harassment for insubordination. She received a CBI notice charging her with holding large illegal property which she claims she does not have any knowledge of. Being a lawyer herself, she was able to fight it out, in spite of the pressure exerted by the CM.

Narendar Kanwar, another independent member of the Assembly, held a number of portfolios in the Bhairon Singh Shekhawat Ministry, Tourism as well as Women and Child Welfare. She was firmly rooted in, and subscribed to, upper-caste attitudes towards women's issues and allegiances to tradition, custom and the Chief Minister. According to her, "historically women are the stronger sex and *sati* is an example of it. When a woman comes under the influence of *sat* (a powerful emotion), the state of mind is such that one can immolate oneself. Nobody can stop a woman who has decided to commit *sati*. My grandmother did it and nobody could stop her. The Press said a lot of negative things during the Roop Kanwar *sati* but this is because they do not understand the tradition behind it. There are also many men who give up on life and pleasure when their wife dies."

However, she was clearly more sympathetic on the Bhanwari Devi issue and like Shashi Dutta, felt that she should be given relief. In fact, she arranged some monetary relief and asserted that the CM was sympathetic to the issue. At the same time she supported the government decision to bring about change in the WDP that would change the focus from dealing with issues of social change to providing economic empowerment. "The *saathin* project was a temporary measure taken by the Rajasthan Government to spread awareness but we have to now ensure that these women do not get dependent on their salaries. Moreover, the project was limited to employing a few hundred women while we now aim to substitute it with economic empowerment programmes. We want to prevent a situation like the Bhanwari incident arising in the future, so we have decided to organise women into groups who would work as a financial unit. The women in a group can propose a scheme (e.g. dairy) and we will provide the funding after examining its validity." Economic empowerment was also seen within the traditional concept of home-related occupations. The aim is thus clear—to steer the question of women's employment away from a path that may lead it to question the nature and rationale of caste and gender oppression.

The most evasive and hostile response to our questions on the kind of space his party and government gave women came from the Chief Minister, **Bhairon Singh Shekhawat,** himself.

He avoided responding on the Bhanwari Devi case on the grounds that it was sub-judice, but gave vent to his feelings on the question of 33 per cent reservation of seats for women in no uncertain (in fact both, hostile and offensive) terms. He almost brushed aside our question of why there were no women Ministers in the government and in positions of authority in the party. "Now with 33 per cent reservation you women will be getting your rights, so use it, what are you asking me about giving women greater participation? I have two women Ministers, so what if they are independent? We can see that women have come up in Panchayat, so you have got what you want."

Unlike the Chief Minister, women Vidhan Sabha members were very positive about the issue of 33 per cent reservation. According to **Shashi Dutta**, women elected to the Panchayat had started a positive trend but there was a need for more educated and professional women to come into politics. At the village level, she felt that the women were uneducated and often controlled by their men. "However, they are attempting to assert themselves and we must support them. Recently there was an event when the CM decided to dismiss two women Panchayat members because they had become pregnant again despite already having several children. I intervened and explained to him, that this action would only dishearten the women. One must remember that the choice of being pregnant in our society is not with the woman. Would you dismiss a man if he had many children and his wife was pregnant again ?"

Kavita Shrivastav, claims that in areas where the NGOs are active there is greater awareness and the women who have come into Panchayats are relatively more independent. For them the positive aspect is that women are coming out in the open and asserting themselves. "Moreover, due to years of subjugation, economic and social pressure women can be more sensitive to the problems of water, electricity and have a tendency to be less corrupt."

Although not very large in terms of numbers, the influence the Rajputs have wielded over Rajasthani society has been substantial. Even today, events such as *sati* capture the imagination of the populace as they are influenced and backed by economic and political power. However, the condition of Rajput women is dismal within the prescribed parameters of a feudal and decadent society. Their position even today in relation to the power equation within the family and society and in terms of an awareness of their disadvantaged position is even worse than the lower-caste women.

Hansa Rajpal, a teacher of political science at Kanaudi College, Jaipur and one of the two Rajput women who came out in support of the anti-*sati* agitation felt that "In Rajasthani society there is no importance given to women's issues. Even when an issue is raised, women from the BJP never join. During the *sati* incident I faced tremendous hostility when I joined the anti-*sati* movement. Being a Rajput, I was accused of being disloyal to my community. Tremendous pressure was put on my family by relatives to stop me. In fact at one stage my husband and, mainly, my son were very angry with me for participation in the anti-*sati* agitation. They felt that there was no need for me to get involved and antagonise the community. But my daughter who saw me on TV rang me up to congratulate me." For the younger generation it became a question of community identity and women like Rani Chundawati (an 80 year-old veteran legislator) had to face public abuse for her anti-*sati* position. The situation according to her has not changed substantially over the years.

The BJP has thrived on conservative religious and caste prejudices backed up by the feudal ethos prevailing in the state. The question of women's participation indirectly questions this structure, that is why despite the party's commitment to 33 per cent reservation for women in Assembly and Parliament, partymen are feeling not only threatened but cornered. This can be seen clearly in the hostility towards women who question the lack of adequate representation and the negative attitude towards reservation itself.

At the same time there was a certain apathy to take up arms and confront the party on issues of non- representation or other women's issues at the State level (as was clearly visible by the response of Ujwala Arora in Rajasthan), despite certain visible resistance at the national level. The hostility of male party members towards the demand for greater representation of women was more articulated at the State level and and there was less hesitancy to go on the record that they were not in favour of such a reservation for women. At the State level, caste identity assumed greater importance and was the deciding factor on the kind of position political parties took on issues relating to women as was clear by the Bhanwari Devi case, the BJP Government in the State did not want to allienate the Gujjar community and lose their vote bank. It became immaterial that such caste configurations, be it the Rajputs in the case of *sati* or the Gujjars in the case of Bhanwari Devi, were the greatest perpetuators of women's oppression, as long as they could be utilised to win elections.

If we look at BJP organisationally, in the past as well as now, very few women from women's wing occupy important party positions within the BJP, and even the prominence accorded to the Rajmata has been more decorative than influential. The women's wing plays hardly any role in the BJP's scheme of things, and whatever importance it has acquired in the recent past is in response to a change in the context rather than a change in the BJP's values or intention. The change in the BJP strategy in order to appeal to the liberal and democratic sections of society does not explicitly envisage the political empowerment of women both within and without the party, as it favours a notion of change that conforms to a tradition that denies women political power. Even this limited change is more perceptible at the national level, the States are yet to feel its impact.

Despite this background, women politicians of the BJP did express concern about the limited access to power that women have both within and outside the party. Significantly, all our interviewees were united in their support for 33 per cent reservation of seats for women in Parliament , as they felt that experience had shown that it was the only way for women to have access to political power.

It is interesting also to see how the Congress is characterised by its vacillating ambiguous positions. At times because of this vacillation it lost the political advantage that it may have achieved if it had reacted with promptness and conviction, as in the case of the Anti-Sati Act. Women in the Congress as in the BJP are not allowed much say even on issues about which they feel strongly. Since there is no ideological position, perceived petty party interests rule over wider considerations of women's welfare. The AIDWA emerges as the only women's organisation with political links which has taken an active and consistent stand on women's issues in Rajasthan. Coordinating and networking with NGOs, it has been giving issue-based support to all manner of women's groups and has contributed towards politicising the women's movement.

Communist Party of India (Marxist) 6

In this chapter we trace the development of the Communist Party of India (Marxist)'s (henceforth CPI(M)) political position on women's issues. Two distinct phases can be identified in this—the first is the period of the 1940s till the 1980s, and the second is the period thereafter, marked by the emergence of the All India Democratic Women's Association (AIDWA).

The CPI(M)'s analysis of the development of society perceives it as class struggle, holding the economic system to be the main foundation of society. "This materialist concept of history and the analysis of the historical development of human society shows that neither exploitation of one class by another, nor the subjugation of women in society is an eternal phenomenon. The inequality between men and women, the subjugation and the inferior status of women in society, also developed through evolution of society at certain stages with class exploitation and will disappear at the higher stage of society where there will be no exploitation." Thus "Marxist interpretation of social relations and social development relates the women's question with universal historical development and universally applicable social laws, and it shows that like all other institutions, the form of the family and the relationship between man and woman are also subject to constant processes

> The inequality between men and women, the subjugation and the inferior status of women in society, also developed through evolution of society at certain stages with class exploitation and will disappear at the higher stage of society where there will be no exploitation.

of change with changes in economic conditions and production relations."[1]

The subjugation of women is seen to coincide with the beginning of class exploitation in society ". . . under the patriarch, when the family was based on private property owned by man, the household work of women lost its public character and the woman, being pushed out of productive labour, was virtually turned into man's private property and domestic slave. This master-slave relationship between man and woman degraded the position of women throughout the stages of class-ridden society, e.g., slavery, feudalism and capitalism... [So it sees] ..... the modern individual family as based on the open or disguised domestic enslavement of the woman: and the modern society is constituted solely of individual families as its molecules."[2]

This perspective holds that the emancipation of women is possible only through their participation in production on a large scale, with domestic duties requiring their attention only to a minor degree.[3] Modern large-scale production provides women with that opportunity, as it brings them out of the family to the labour market, with the result that women no longer have to be financially dependent on men and can contribute and maintain the family. "Under large-scale industry and bourgeois enlightenment, when some sections of women come out of the four walls of the family to seek employment, education and legal social rights, we see that they start marching towards emancipation under whatever difficulty there may be."[4]

1 Mukherjee, Kanak, *Women's Emancipation Movement in India*, National Book Centre, 1989.

2 *Ibid.*

3 Obviously, this is not held to be true for the entire society. Only a small number among the industrial labour force are able to avail of this advantage, since most other women continue to live within extremely exploitative relationships.

4 This does not mean that women did not participate in agricultural production and were not an important part of the agricultural labour force; it only assumes industrial production as a higher form of production relations and hence as having greater potential for liberating women. (Mukherjee, *Women's Emancipation Movement in India*.)

But because capitalism sustains exploitative relationships, full emancipation is possible only under socialism: "For centuries the civilised world assumed the inferior position of women in society and also sometimes tried to redress their hardship. But it is only the Marxist doctrine that dug deep into the root cause of the exploitation and the inferior position of women in society. It showed that it was not an eternal social system or any divine order that made the women subordinate to men, but it was the evolution of class society and the class exploitation that is at the root of all discrimination against women. That the fate of the oppressed women in the society is inseparably bound up with the fate of all other oppressed sections of the people and especially the working class who were to champion the social revolution".[5]

However, it has been argued that this viewing of women's emancipation strictly within the sphere of class struggle, has proved to be too restrictive. Consequently, for many years the party failed to recognise the oppression faced by women due to social and religious traditions that went far beyond class categories. There was also a failure to recognise women's problems as separate and distinct from other marginalised sections, and that they carried the double burden of both caste and class oppression.

Mahila Raksha Samiti

In order to focus on the women within the CPI(M) it is important to go into the history of the women's movement within the Communist movement. An examination of the growth and evolution of the Mahila Raksha Samiti in West Bengal can help us identify some central tendencies. The united Communist Party took the initiative to form a democratic mass organisation of all toiling women. Until then, though these women had participated in workers' and peasants' movements,

[5] *Ibid.*

there had been no real separate platform or organisation for them. Organisations like the AIWC, etc., represented only the educated upper strata of women.

The forties saw many mass organisations of women getting together to fight fascism.[6] Among these the most prominent was the Mahila Atma-Raksha Samiti (MARS). The MARS held its first meeting in 1942 with only 112 members but by 1944 its membership had grown to about 43,500. Initially it was primarily involved in rehabilitation of poor rural and urban women after the Bengal famine and relief work through kitchens and first-aid centres; it also organised demonstrations against black-marketeers and hoarders. Though it was claimed that the main force of the MARS were the toiling masses, it was nevertheless a very broad patriotic platform for women from all walks of life who were concerned with the defence of the country against fascism and about famine relief. Hence even women belonging to the Hindu Mahasabha were associated with the MARS. However, the political leadership remained with the CPI.

Since the thirties there have been big peasants' movements in Bengal and many other provinces in India, in all of which women participated in large numbers. The role of women and their extraordinary militancy in the Tebhaga movement (1946-48) led by sharecroppers who demanded two-thirds of the crop (instead of one half of the crop) deserve special mention. Women formed *Nari Bahinis* (women's militia) which confronted landlords, encircled the police and forcibly harvested the paddy. They also played an important role in organising communication by transmitting messages between activists, hiding cadres who had gone underground, and raising the alarm when the police came. Tribal women and widows emerged from their normal seclusion to play an important role

6 The reference here to facism is in the context of the World War and the support of Indian Communists of the Allies (which included the Soviet Union) when the Congress was not willing to support the British war effort unless they gave certain concessions to the Indian nationalists.

(Rájbansis, Bimal Maji). The MARS, however, played a relatively minor role in the Tebhaga movement, largely because of its urban middle-class composition and its distance from poor rural women. In the early stages of the Tebagha movement, the CPI was in its radical phase and did not discourage women's spontaneous protest. After 1947, when the CPI appealed to the peasants to reject direct action and rely upon legal channels, women's militancy seems to have subsided.

After independence the democratic women's movement, according to Kanak Mukherjee, entered a new phase of struggle, as the Congress Government that assumed power represented the bourgeois-landlord classes and attacked the working class and the peasantry. The legacies of colonialism and feudalism continued to exist in independent India, as did the exploitation of workers and peasants and the middle classes. There was no basic change in the condition of women. They remained victims of class exploitation and the feudal legacies of backward and superstitious customs, bigotry, and religious fundamentalism, in spite of the pious declarations of the Constitution. Kanak Mukherjee identifies the unchanged nature of land relations as the primary factor in ensuring that the basic causes of women's inferior status were not removed.

The Communist Party of India was banned in 1948. Widespread mass struggles took place; the Tebhaga movement in the villages, and the textile and mine workers' movements in the city grew. The Congress Government tried to suppress these movements. The government oppression was directed not only against the CPI but also against its mass organisations. The MARS, along with many other mass organisations, was banned and it worked underground between 1947 and 1951. During this period, it encountered massive onslaughts: the police killed four Communist women at a demonstration in Calcutta in April 1949; numerous women were killed in the district through this period; many women leaders were imprisoned for long periods of time without trial. As a result of this repression, membership of the MARS dwindled sharply, and it was completely isolated. It was only in 1952 under considerable pressure from mass movements and the Habeas Corpus case that the ban on the CPI and other organisations including the MARS was lifted.

As mentioned earlier, till 1949, the Communist women had participated in the Congress party affiliated All India Women's Congress (AIWC), but from then on, as was only to be expected, the AIWC took sides with the Congress Government. Thereafter, the AIWC confined its activity to some social work and some propaganda work for women's rights, while the MARS and other democratic organisations continued their struggle against the Congress Government. As a result of these differences, the Communist and other Left-oriented women felt the need for a separate platform and formed the National Federation of Indian Women (NFIW) in 1954. Vidya Munshi claims that the Communist men initially opposed the formation of the NFIW for they feared it would divide and weaken the party but the women overcame their resistance. The NFIW poured its energies into constructive activities and established contact with women's organisations of the Communist bloc. The NFIW became affiliated with the Soviet-based international organisation, the Women's International Democratic Federation, which did not espouse independent feminist goals.[7]

In 1953, the MARS was reconstituted as the Paschim Banga Mahila Samiti (PBMS) and became the most important constituent of the NFIW in West Bengal. The Communist women's movement was further disrupted by the split of the Communist Party in 1964 into the CPI and the CPI(M), although women members of the PBMS continued to work together until

[7] Besides the struggle against the Congress Government, the fifties and the sixties are marked by the growth of the democratic women's movement and the establishment of international linkages which were to have a far-reaching influence on the agenda of the women's movement in the years to come. This phase is also marked by the inclusion of the middle class in the coalition of workers and peasants.

1971. Relations became strained after the CPI(M)-led government in the State was brought down in the same year.[8] The PBMS remained affiliated with the CPI, whereas the Paschim Banga Gantantric Mahila Samiti (PBGMS) was established as a separate organisation affiliated with the CPI(M). The PBGMS born out of the split was considered to be more sectarian than its predecessor. The contrast between the two Communist women's organisations became particularly marked after the Left Front came to power in 1977. The CPI-affiliated PBMS joined other feminist groups in struggling against women's oppression, but the PBGMS, because of its close links with the government, was often not in a position to do so.

During this period both the AIWC and the NFIW were forced to compromise on various women's issues because of political and ideological proximity with the Congress Government. Even when these issues directly affected the interests of women they were in no position to assert themselves. Individually many women opposed the position of the Congress Government but politically they were in no position to take a public stand or go against the party. Neither of these organisations, according to Kanak Mukherjee, were for radical change of society or ready to oppose the Congress.

Debate with Feminism

The early CPI(M) response to feminism was often dismissive, and sometimes downright hostile. Since they tend not to recognise the diversity in the feminist movement and view it as a monolithic entity, the Marxists took issue with what they perceived to be feminism's inability to view the women's question in relation to class struggle. The CPI(M) disagrees with

[8] It must be recalled that this was a period of CPI collaboration with the Congress Government and that it was the Central Government which connived to bring down the duly elected government in West Bengal.

the view that exploitation of women in society is due primarily to patriarchy, the solution to which lies in women of all classes of society coming together to fight men. Their assumption that feminists are not concerned about the question of class has been challenged by the feminists. The feminists, on their part, feel that the Marxists avoid addressing the issue of patriarchal relationships, pointing out that women's emancipation has not necessarily been coterminus with class struggle. As societies have progressed from one stage of historical development to another, the position of women has not significantly altered for the better, and the same situation appears to exist in a number of socialist countries. Some feminists, therefore, argue for a feminist perspective within socialism, as it has not been able to overcome the limitations of patriarchy, and in fact has built other structures that make the struggle against patriarchy more difficult.

The Marxists, in response, argue that socialist societies have achieved a level of equality between the sexes that is quite unparalleled in history, and due precisely to the understanding that the struggle for gender justice and equality of opportunity must proceed hand-in-hand with class struggle. For, "the proletarian revolution and the party of the working class helps men and women to get rid of ideas of male domination by political education (the fact that gender sensitisation hardly figures in the party's ideological education is conveniently overlooked). Trade unions, women's wing of the trade unions, women's organisations fight against the male domination expressed in every field in socialist countries."[9]

Marxist women activists view as dubious the refusal by many feminist organisations to mobilise women on broader

9 In our view, this defence of the position of women in socialist countries is naive, and erroneous when suggested as a model for the women's movement in India. At best we can say that initially among the newly emergent socialist states there was a valiant attempt to address the issues pertaining to equality of women in all spheres. But as the euphoria of the revolution waned so did the good intentions and what re-emerged was the tendency to revert to patriarchally established traditional roles.

> The contribution of feminists in focusing and raising questions of discrimination against women cannot be overlooked or trivialised, especially if it is interpreted as a struggle for the just distribution of power that men of all classes disproportionately enjoy.

socio-economic issues. This kind of conflict can be seen to come to the fore for example on the question of joint action (1982) on dowry deaths, price rise, attacks on women in various states, etc. Since the feminists would not consider price rise as an issue specific to women, but as an issue relating to all sections of society, they do not see the need for active participation of women. For the Marxists, a position that believes women to be isolated from overall deprivation is highly questionable and some of them have even analysed feminism as an imperialist conspiracy to divide the working-class movement. This perception has been strengthened by the sudden emergence of NGOs in many third world countries with lots of money to take up the cause of women. Initially, most of these organisations were marked by an antipathy towards political parties, who they felt were incapable and unwilling to address the problems of women and other downtrodden sections. The Marxists took issue[10] with the model of apolitical development espoused by the NGOs, and a serious debate between the two views developed.[11]

In our view, it would be more constructive for the various groups in the women's movement to be more self-critical, as it is frequently the case that the discourse on the women's question locates the goal of gender equality in some future

10 Feminists and Women's Movement by Vimal Ranadive, as well as numerous articles by feminists that have appeared in the press, attacking the Left Parties and governments.

11 Many of these differences still persist, but increasingly both groups have come to recognise the need for unity in the Indian context, especially on issues such as the rise of fundamentalism.

utopian society. The questions that every political ascription that professes the women's cause must address are quite straightforward as they pertain to the here-and-now: How far is the concern for gender equality reflected in the day-to-day functioning of democratic politics? It must be noted that the question of political participation in decision-making is a complex and delicate one, as the objective is not seizure of power from men, but of democratisation of power. Furthermore, have political parties subscribing to the view that class struggle brings with it gender awareness actually been able to bring that kind of awareness among both male and female party workers? Have they been able to ensure that their words and deeds are consistent with their professed aims of women's emancipation? An instructive example is the discourse around the Left-led price-rise agitation mentioned above — why should women be more concerned than men about price rise, just because they run the kitchen? Within Marxist ideology emancipation means the liberation of women from the drudgery of domestic work, but by structuring its arguments in this fashion, the Left reinforces the commonly held assumption that the kitchen is (and should be) the woman's primary concern. Thus the feminists would argue that the main divide between them and AIDWA is centred round the ways in which they perceive women's identity in the public and domestic spheres.

The contribution of feminists in focusing and raising questions of discrimination against women cannot be overlooked or trivialised, especially if it is interpreted as a struggle for the just distribution of power that men of all classes now disproportionately enjoy. Simultaneously, the Marxist demand for ideological and political moorings for the women's movement is an equally justified one. It is now increasingly recognised that political parties are more responsive to the needs of women both within and outside the party only when there is a strong woman's movement to back up women's demands. As the Communist-led women's movement has shown, the history of prolonged struggles has both sensitised women as well as strengthened their role both within and outside the party, and being part of a wider democratic movement has given them a definite sense of direction and values.

The Birati Rape Case

Tanika Sarkar in her article, "Reflections on Birati Rape Case: Gender Ideology in Bengal",[12] raises certain very important issues in relation to the professed ideology of the Marxists and its praxis when it comes to issues related to women. Sarkar suggests the fact that the Bengali self-image has been closely dependent on the nationalist construction of notions of woman and womanhood.[13] It has led to the assimilation of these notions into the ideology

[12] "Reflections on Birati Rape Case:Gender Ideology in Bengal", *Economic and Political Weekly*, 2 February 1991. The article was structured around the gang-rape of three Bangladeshi refugee women in Birati, West Bengal on 17 July 1990.

[13] Hardening nationalism rejected the critique of the reform movement, apart from the one of submitting to foreign rule. "Women lost their signifying power as metaphors of actual social evil to become metaphors of latent social greatness. Attainment of this iconic stature ('jewels of the country') put a closure on self-critical probing into their real conditions within nationalism, and led to the acceptance of the traditional Bengali perception of womanhood — the deified woman is essentially a mother figure who attains her highest possibilities as a symbol of the motherland. Motherhood is not so much biological as a characterological trait, potential for nurture, for self-sacrifice, for unquestioning giving. It is an inner faculty that irradiates the notion of feminine love and beauty in any form. The mother was always an invocation against loss. If colonialism was the loss of control over the self and the sources of its nurture, deprivation from food, wealth and power, then the most poignant and contestatory image of the loss would be the separation of the child from the mother."

The suffering of women that marked this period of famines, riots and partition (of Bengal), "all that would remain of that image would be the loving woman whose unfailing bounty had to sustain an entire people through the holocaust. Women were perhaps the worst victims of these catastrophes but Bengal needed them as a source of comfort and strength, not as victims." The prescriptive uni-dimensionality of this mother image kept out other more active and assertive images.

of the Left in West Bengal.[14] This special relation between Bengal and its women has not, however, resulted in efforts to ensure better health, education, marital conditions, general opportunities, etc. for women, but has manifested itself only "in terms of the nebulous, pervasive concept of a deep respect for women – that is, as a state of the male attitude rather than a specific feature in women's existence or consciousness." Such images influence our perception of issues and situations, and she takes the CPI(M)'s initial response to the Birati rape case and Shyamali Gupta's (PBGMS) initial statement to illustrate this relationship.

> Pre-independence ideologies of cultural nationalism engendered an enduring image of women.

Sarkar strongly feels the Left Front viewed the issue in terms of this unified tradition, and subscribed to the enduring elements within it. Since Bengalis and Bengali culture are not like that, the horrible crime had to be committed by criminals. In order to cope with this fact, one must divide society into the good guys and the bad guys, criminal space and the normal segment, and Gupta's statement was an attempt to do just that. The statement seeks first to establish that the victims were women of easy morals (they enjoyed sexual relations with more than one man), and then argues that the men they are alleged to have had relationships with were anti-social elements. It is thus implied that the rape was perfectly understandable.

Besides the fact that Gupta uses middle-class norms of morality, rather than the yardstick of law, to evaluate the crime,

[14] This has also been discussed in Chapter 2. The Left not only assimilated the earlier tradition, reaching out for self-fulfilment was ruled out, perhaps because it was also seen as a translation of 'bourgeois individualism', as self-centredness or selfishness. Non-domestic, non-party roles were seen as products of tragic necessity at best, not as liberation. Much of the Left discourse at rallies recasts party roles into familial roles. Any woman who extends beyond such a role is to be feared.

her statement also implies that it is only certain categories of women who get raped. "The only relevance of such a description resides in the unstated assumption that there are degrees of culpability in a crime like rape, that women require certain sexual and property qualification to be classified as fully legitimate rape victims." The statement thus alters the basic terms of discussion, by describing the victims as prostitutes, and reading prostitution not as victimisation of women but as criminality. Sarkar concludes by asking for a review of the Left culture in Bengal, for the CPI(M)'s position on the issue clearly indicates a retreat from the prescriptions its ideology makes about gender as well as class.

Brinda Karat, Central Committee Member of the CPI(M), responding to Sarkar's criticism,[15] declared that the Left has never claimed infallibility or lack of weakness in gender insight, but she would also like to see whether such sharp criticism could be levelled at the CPI(M)'s stand on the issues confronting the women's movement today. She says that Shyamali Gupta's statement must be seen as an aberration and does not reflect the AIDWA's or the party's stand (thereby accepting that it was a prejudicial statement), and refers to the mass mobilisation which took place against the Birati case and the attempt to sensitise public opinion so that such cases did not occur in the future.

Karat's response notwithstanding, the issue of how pre-independence ideologies of cultural nationalism engendered an enduring image of women that Sarkar raises is an important one. We had noted its role earlier in the Congress and BJP's perception of women in politics and society, and we now see that this legacy has been inherited by the Left as well. This nationalist discourse is overlapping, and tends to blur the wider politics when it comes to women.

15 "On Birati, the CPI(M) and Tradition in Bengal", *Economic and Political Weekly*, 4 May 1991.

Failure of Revolutionary Politics

Extensive criticism has been levelled at the old CPI and later the CPI(M) for not fulfilling its revolutionary potential for the betterment of women both within the party and in society. Focusing primarily on the CPI(M), Amrita Basu, in her book *Two Faces of Protest*[16] feels that the CPI(M) women activists have lost their militancy to a large extent when compared with the Shramik Sangh activism in Maharashtra. Pointing out that CPI(M) leaders have frequently orchestrated women's demonstrations, such as the PBGMS anti-famine demonstration in Bankura district in 1977, she suggests that women in the organisation have been given little autonomy. This was evident in the fact that no Left-led agitation against the State Government has been launched in West Bengal.

Basu claims that from 1977 onwards, the CPI(M) has devoted greater priority to attaining and maintaining power, and this in turn has meant that the expansion of its membership and that of its mass organisations has increasingly become an end in itself. The PBGMS especially was used as a vehicle for securing votes. It was simultaneously discouraged from organising any agitational movements, as the need to reconcile the different class, gender, and ethnic interests of the CPI(M) constituency became paramount. Furthermore, the CPI(M) became less responsive to women, who now constituted only one part of a large and heterogeneous constituency. This sacrifice of ideology to electoral compulsions, Basu holds, has resulted in a "*bhadralok* (urban, educated, upper-caste) character of the party, which is often reflected in its moralistic middle-class position on various issues related to women".

"The essence of Stalinist communism," argues Ronald Tiersky,[17] "is its monolithic internal politics." If we extend

[16] Oxford University Press, 1993.

[17] Basu, Amrita, *Two Faces of Protest*, Oxford University Press, 1993.

the realm of internal Communist party politics where democratic centralist principles are already prefigured, into the private sphere, like the CPI(M), the Bengali Hindu family is organised along strictly hierarchical lines: the men who occupy the highest rung exercise the most power. Yet the family, like the party, mystifies such inequality and projects itself as a solidaristic unit whose members share identical interests. Democratic centralist principles fortify the CPI(M) in the world, at the cost of perpetual sexual inequality. Basu alleges that, "rather than challenging women's subordination CPI(M) has built upon it. Tacit acceptance of female seclusion, which as stated earlier has its roots in upper-caste traditions, benefits the CPI(M) in many ways : it accords with CPI(M)'s attempt to create a cross-class coalition in which middle-class interest will predominate. The stability of women's role as wives and mothers reassure those who fear radical change and demonstrates the CPI(M)'s sympathy for traditional practices. Most importantly by accepting the roles that Bengali Hindu society prescribes for women, the CPI(M) can demonstrate its allegiance to Bengali cultural identity in the face of pervasive fear of domination by the Hindi-speaking heartland."

This acceptance of women's subordination within the family may well be subscribed to by the CPI(M), but the Communist movement has not always done so. Basu observes, "As sectarian as it might have been in its early stages, the CPI was far more willing to challenge 'bourgeois practices' that included traditional gender relations than the CPI(M) is today." Given the formidable barriers they had to overcome, Communist women were more audacious in the 1940s than they are today perhaps because they had been active in the so-called terrorist movements, a violent anti-imperialist struggle, in the first two decades of the twentieth century. Moreover, clearly they struggled harder to resolve the contradictions between their public and private roles. Although the Communists have always been drawn from the *bhadralok* (most young women who joined the Communist movement during the early period were from wealthy, conservative families), their identification with middle-class interests and commitment to electoral success have grown simultaneously. However, even during that period the reality is that the CPI never seriously challenged sexual inequality, cultivated female leadership, or addressed the problems of poor rural women.

One can only speculate as to why such a chasm grew between the party member's private and public lives. The period of long association during the freedom struggle with the Congress, which was strongly marked by this middle-class approach may have influenced a non-critical approach to gender relations and acceptance of a cultural nationalist formula that sees the woman as the repository of traditional Indian culture. Vidya Munshi[18] has described the AIWC as an important national forum in which the Communists could disseminate their ideas, make contact with otherwise inaccessible women, and influence relevant legislation. Munshi claims that the Communist women, until their withdrawal in 1949, transformed the AIWC from an urban-elite organisation into a mass organisation. Nevertheless, the Communist women may have paid a heavy price for this association with non-Congress women, imbibing middle-class attitudes of women's role in the family and in society. The much admired role models of the time were often women who contributed substantially to the national movement but never questioned conventional cultural roles; as a result, the euphoria and romance of the freedom struggle prevented the Communist women from radicalising the struggle in their own interest. Strategy and tactics for national freedom took precedence over other concerns.

The entry of the CPI(M) and CPI into electoral politics may

[18] "Communists in the Indian Women's Movement".

also have created contradictions between professed beliefs and the day-to-day compromises required to survive in the game of votes and vote-banks. **Gita Mukherjee**, commenting on the CPI, says that it seems to have increasingly absorbed dominant cultural values once it was incorporated into the formal political arena, and she traces the cause of this decline to the acceptance of electoral politics by the party. She is of the view that from 1950 onwards the CPI undermined the autonomy of mass organisations and other groups by relying on them for electoral mobilisation. More broadly, in West Bengal as in other contexts, women's activism tended to be confined to periods of political crisis. In the absence of revolutionary upheaval, women were not compelled to "perform men's jobs in fields, factory, or battlegrounds." But even in its hey-day the CPI was ill-equipped to challenge gender inequality, particularly among poor rural women. There was a deep cultural divide between urban, educated, upper-class Communist leaders and the rural poor.

Amrita Basu also critiques the CPI(M)'s failure to generate income and employment opportunities for women. Consider first its initial position on land redistribution, which was essentially a progressive measure. Pointing out that many progressive steps no longer appear as progressive when the issue of gender is given serious consideration, Basu argues that even while land redistribution advances the interest of the male peasantry which has traditionally been an extremely exploited section, it may actually widen gender inequalities if women do not receive land titles as well. In refusing to implement its own ideology of linking women's limited inheritance rights to the progress of women, the CPI(M) actually worsened the economic disparity between men and women by bestowing land titles on the usually male heads of households. Similarly, hardly any measures were taken to protect and generate women's employment, and in fact certain employment schemes led to the unemployment or underemployment of women even as men gained.[19] Wherever employment opportunities have been created for women, they were in such home-based forms of production as knitting, sewing and weaving.

Basu contends that on the question of increasing and extending women's political participation, the performance of the party has been equally bad. There were only two women in the 1982-87 Left Front Government, and both were low-ranking Ministers with 'soft' portfolios—Minister for Relief and Social Welfare and Minister of State for Education. In the 1987-92 government, only one of the 32 Cabinet Ministers was a woman, Chhay Bera, who was allocated Relief, one of the weakest ministries in the government. This under-representation in the Cabinet was specially surprising, given the relatively large number of women elected to the Vidhan Sabha in that election. Suggestions at the time for a Ministry on Women were opposed by the AIDWA and PBGMS as they felt that the Welfare Ministry adequately covered the needs of women. They cautioned against an artificial separation of the problems of women and that of men. At the local level as well, women's representation has not been significant. In 1978, the Left Front Government decreed that at least two Panchayat members should be women. The government was supposed to nominate members if they were not elected in the general balloting, but still women remained under-represented. Although the position improved slightly by the third Panchayat elections (1988), a large number of the women who sit in Panchayats even today have to be nominated rather than elected.

This under-representation is evident even within the party organisation. There are no women in the Politburo, and the number of women has increased from four to just five in the

[19] The PBGMS has also failed to demand that women should be recognised as share-croppers in their own right. Amrita Basu quotes Shyamali Gupta, its Secretary, as saying that the people would not accept that women work as hard as men.

Central Committee; the same holds true in every State Committee and district-level committee. When questioned on the issue by Amrita Basu, Kanak Mukherjee dismissed the problem of women's invisibility: "Women's political participation should not be measured by counting heads, the more important question is how active are women in political struggle." Other leaders, both male and female, have also maintained this position, pointing out that having a woman Prime Minister had not changed anything for the women of this country. It appears that the CPI(M) refuses to accept the fact that female visibility in the political arena establishes their identity as social actors, even though the women who come to occupy political office need not necessarily represent the interests of women. This becomes extremely important in an environment that still does not consider the public sphere a legitimate sphere for women.

The CPI(M) has thus tended to ignore, under-represent, and even disparage women's interests. At the simplest level of analysis, male and female leaders are often oblivious to the varied manifestations of sexual inequality. The leadership, especially the males, simply do not consider women's issues to be serious political questions. A common strategy of prevarication is the use of Engels' maxim that women's emancipation is contingent upon socialism, as this can be used to justify inaction. Coordination with feminist movements is also impossible, as subscribing to any other category except class is thought to be divisive to the working-class movement. The CPI(M)'s adherence to Marxism has been most doctrinaire and least adaptive to Indian realities where women, caste and tribal struggles are concerned. The party has paid amply for the mistake *vis-a-vis* caste, as now the allegiance of the lower castes has shifted to caste-based parties who were willing to recognise the unique features of lower-caste discrimination, un-analysable in terms of pure class analysis. It is time that the CPI(M) realises that the discrimination against women is also recalcitrant to an analysis along class lines, for if it does not, it must prepare to surrender the leadership of the women's movement to an apolitical NGO women's movement.

It has often been claimed that the subordination of women is primarily social, whereas that of men is economic, and therefore a Communist Party may be expected to give primacy to economic issues over social concerns, however pressing the need. Such distinctions obscure the intimate relations between the two spheres of society and the economy, but women leaders in the CPI(M) have frequently adopted this analysis. As a consequence, and ironically, the more competent and recognised a woman is within the party, the less time she has for dealing with the issues of women. The older generation of leaders would think it disparaging to think of themselves as representing primarily the interests of women. The struggles that the PBGMS took up during 1980-85 reveals the attitude of the party to its women's organisations and the use it puts these organisations to: State autonomy *vis-a-vis* the Centre, higher prices for agricultural produce, equal wages, reduced inflation and global peace. Thus, with a few exceptions, rural woman had no opportunity to organise around the specific problems they confront in their daily lives.

Electoral politics and the acceptance of the traditional family as the norm are two other important factors that have contributed to a bias against women in the Communist movement. In most Communist countries, including China, parties have made concessions to patriarchal morality to facilitate acceptance of its mass-politics line. In India, as well, the CPI(M) fears male opposition if women were to acquire independent land-holdings, and fears being voted out if it were to propose far-reaching reforms of the religious laws that govern the family. So it seeks to avoid these questions by dismissing their relevance.

Party organisation and hierarchy also militate against

growth in the importance of women's organisations. The structures in place ensure (a) the continued subordination of the PBGMS to the CPI(M); (b) inequality between the urban middle-class PBGMS leaders and poor rural women; and (c) the perpetuation of female members in subordinate positions within the party hierarchy. Often many of the CPI(M) women are married to men who are active in the CPI(M) and who generally out-rank their wives. Democratic centralism perhaps extends to the home, and ensures that the PBGMS members are unlikely to challenge the party, since doing so would require them to question the superiority of male party members as well as their own husbands. The CPI(M) is hardly in a position to create greater public acceptance of women when it upholds their traditional roles in both the party and the family.

Changing with the times: AIDWA

Since the 1980s, there has been a perceptible change in the CPI(M)'s attitude to the women's question. The 1982 Party Congress identified women's struggles "as not just a struggle for social reform but an integral part of the Indian people's struggle for democracy and socialism." The same Congress passed a resolution that stated that membership to the All India Democratic Women's Association[20] would be open to non-party members as well. Within West Bengal, the Left Front Government gave party tickets to 16 women to contest the Assembly elections in 1987, 14 were elected, of whom 12 were from the CPI(M). But the efforts are

[20] Under the umbrella of the CPI(M), the party works through mass organisations in different sections of society, e.g., students, workers, women, etc. The All India Democratic Women's Association is such a mass front for women. It is inappropriate to call it the women's wing of the party because not all members of the AIDWA are members of the party. However, most office-bearers are members of the party and it generally works within the overall common understanding of the party; this is also the case with the CITU which works on the trade union front.

still not adequate and attitudes to the question of the woman's role both at home and in politics remain largely unchanged under a broad assumption of good intentions. It must also be recognised that these organisations were closely linked through fraternal ties with Communist movements on different fronts throughout the world and were exposed to international pressures to accommodate the issues of women among their concerns.

If the undivided CPI created a counter-community for a small group of urban middle-class women in the 1940s, the CPI(M) has replaced its efforts in the 1980s, this time for rural women. Without doubt, its greatest achievement has been to instill a feeling of dignity in poor rural women through political struggle. They exude an unmistakable sense of solidarity, efficacy and pride in 'their' party that can be seen even at party-sponsored rallies. This feeling grows out of a political context that is relatively free from police repression, caste and 'communal' conflict, and violence against women. The struggle for joint *patta* gave them added strength. In fact, today the PBGMS has drawn up a series of demands addressed to the West Bengal Government asking for concrete action in terms of women's employment and policies for greater empowerment of women in all areas of social economic and political life. The government has already started the process of converting all land deeds to joint patta, that is, joint ownership of land by husband and wife. Reforms are being initiated in the area of employment of women in the unorganised sector. However, there has been no serious questioning of the categories of perception that the Marxists have adopted from the cultural nationalism that arose during the colonial experience.

It was primarily as a response to the "growing revolutionary urge" within the democratic women's movement that the CPI(M) took the initiative to form the All India Democratic Women's Association (AIDWA) in 1981. According to its

Constitution, "All India Democratic Women's Association (AIDWA) takes upon itself the task of organising the masses of women in the towns and villages of India and of building a broad-based women's movement for uplift and betterment of the lot of women as a whole, to remove all discrimination between men and women, to fight for democracy, equal rights and emancipation of women, in a society free from exploitation."

The AIDWA has a broad perspective on the democratic women's movement, and the revolutionary aim of fighting for a radical change of society, towards socialism, when real emancipation of women will be possible. It is categorical in linking the women's struggle to the broader class struggle, and hence extends its full cooperation and support to all progressive and democratic sections of the people. The leadership of the AIDWA is constituted by leaders and workers of the CPI(M).

Although the AIDWA calls for a broad united front to work for the cause of women, it cautions against 'party-less and above party' feminist organisations. These feminists, says Kanak Mukherjee, though of various views, pose the women's question as fundamentally opposed to men and hold the patriarchal system of society as being primarily responsible for the exploitation of women. Thus they try to divert the class struggle into a struggle between men and women. This breeds hatred in the family and conjugal life and leads to isolation of the women's movement.

A growing threat perceived by the AIDWA is of communalism, a threat that makes it imperative for democratic sections to unite. It critiques the Congress for the compromises it has repeatedly made with communal forces, as a result of which these forces have gained substantial strength. The communal forces pose a grave threat to the democratic women's movement, as both Hindu and Muslim communalists are opposed to the democratic rights of women and try to push women back to domestic slavery. This can be seen in the positions taken by them on the question of the Muslim Women's Bill and the *sati* issue. Age-old feudal superstitions, customs and usages, and religious bigotry are spreading among all sections of society. The more women fight against economic and social discrimination and strive for equal rights with men, the more feudal obscurantism stands in their way. The fundamentalists give sanction, through religious garb and glamour, to the inferior and low status of women, and to their conditions of domestic slavery. The AIDWA stresses the need to launch a ceaseless struggle against backward ideologies and customs and to organise a broad-based movement uniting all sections of women to fight against denial of and encroachment on women's rights.

The increased visibility of women in diverse sectors of the economy in post-independence India often makes us oblivious to the fact that this effect has been felt only in certain classes, and that even within these classes women have not been able to overcome certain limitations imposed by conservative religious and social traditions.

The increased visibility of women in diverse sectors of the economy in post-independence India often makes us oblivious to the fact that this effect has been felt only in certain classes, and that even within these classes women have not been able to overcome certain limitations imposed by conservative religious and social traditions. Even legal equality remains unequal due certain personal laws being in force. Recognising this, AIDWA has participated and effectively intervened in protest movements against the Muslim Women's Bill and *sati*. It has been able to coordinate united action with other women's organisations, despite basic differences in understanding, since it aims to form such united platforms on the basis of an immediate programme.

However, a criticism often made in the context of these

changes and the hopes and expectations that they have generated from the organisation (AIDWA) is of vanguardism. It is said this approach tends to limit the relationship between the 'activists' and others to a one-way process. Combined with what is described as "arrogance of knowledge", it creates stumbling blocks in its wider objectives. Theoretical premises rooted in history should not prevent serious engagement with "real" histories. This has resulted in a wrong approach to and understanding of issues like caste and women's identity, and in ignoring certain issues like environment and technology which have been historically crucial to poor rural women. Linked to this is also the concept of a teleological history of "stages" in the development of capitalism which has at times forced them to uncritically accept development policies which in many instances marginalised women.

A Long Struggle: Women of the CPI (M) 7

Marxists and feminists have debated too long whether the socialist countries were able to achieve women's liberation or not, whether the cultural revolution to dismantle feudal structures has been achieved or not. It is erroneous to take the erstwhile socialist countries as a measure of either the success or failure of the Indian Marxist approach. In our analysis of the CPI(M)'s response to the women's question and the political representation of women, we focus on the record of the Marxist parties in empowering women as well as their responsiveness to the growing concern of women for greater access to power both within and outside the party.

In this context, the issue of autonomy of women within parties has been frequently raised. It has been asserted that as men will always remain patriarchal, women's organisations must be controlled only by women and that they must enjoy some measure of autonomy. While this is valid in itself, it raises the question as to whether it is necessarily true that women's organisations working within political parties are always denied autonomy. Such a statement implies, first, that there should be no link between the party's day-to-day functioning and its proclaimed ideological position on women and their role in society, economy and politics. Second, it implies that historically, women of the Left parties have played a limited role because of their subservience to the party, not contributing to empowerment of women either within or without the party. In the interviews that follow, we obtain insights into these issues.

In the context of organisations like the AIDWA, these issues are all the more pertinent. The implication is that the concept of a frontal mass organisation which has an organisational link and relationship with the party is a big hoax. Also that the nature of the relationship of the women's movement and the party remains fixed over time and does not change with changes in the roles that frontal organisations like the AIDWA are required to perform in different historical situations. Both these assumptions can be questioned, as the organisational relationships function through certain established codes, with the nature of control changing according to historical factors.

Another important question that needs to be addressed is: will the Left Parties be able to redress the gender inequality that exists in Indian society, especially when they subsume the problems of women under general questions of class struggle? It is claimed that the strategy employed by the Left is one of prevarication, by which it holds issues of class to be more important, postponing the women's question to a later date. We must look at history to see whether this claim can be substantiated. Has the women's front been neglected by the party? Has the party or any of its affiliated organisations failed to respond to certain issues raised by women's organisations? Has this position been static or has it changed over time? Has the change, if any, come from the benevolence of party bosses or have women within these organisations struggled to bring about this change?

It is interesting to see how women within the CPI(M) view themselves, the party and the issue of under-representation of women in the corridors of power both of the party and the Left Front Government in West Bengal. The responses of the women interviewed revealed the relationship between ideology, history and women's day-to-day experience.

Kanak Mukherjee, a member of the Central Committee of the CPI(M), has literally grown with the party. She joined politics at a very young age (eighteen) in 1938 and became a member of the undivided Communist Party. She started to attend study classes in 1936 and by 1939 she had joined the students' movement. She was an active member of the Student's Federation of India (SFI). She was also active in the underground Communist movement in 1940-42 and was imprisoned several times. She was one of the founders of the Mahila Atma Raksha Samiti in 1943.

She has never felt at a disadvantage in the party and says that women have to change their attitude and help themselves. In order to do this they have to overcome the hesitancy of women in breaking their silence and demanding what is rightfully theirs. According to Mukherjee, this is the main stumbling block in any effective intervention by women to assert their rights. She claims that very often women are more sincere, more devoted to the cause, but they have to be developed. They have to get over their hesitancy. Today, according to her, the political scenario has changed and far more women are visible. She says that even if they are not present in Parliament and the legislatures, they are present in large numbers in the voting lines. Women must be more involved in politics. The traditional, feudal and mental attitudes of men and women has been another major stumbling block. The deprivation faced by women in society over centuries has pushed them back. Reservation of seats has became important today in the context of our failure to draw women and enforce the principle of equality. The people still do not see men and women as equal. She emphasised that although reservation is important, women must, along with it, develop a desire to change. Reservation today is an option as what we expected to happen naturally has not happened.

Mukherjee feels that the issue of the male attitude towards greater participation of women in politics and in positions of power is complex and there is no uniform or universal response. She said that many people are members of the CPI(M), from different regions, cultures and classes. They bring with them their own attitudes, traditions and beliefs, which are often feudal. The party's political aim is that of equality, but often there is discrimination due to the attitudes of the implementors. Within our party there is a constant struggle to change the traditional attitudes of men and women. A major problem is that women often do not raise their voice. They do not assert their rights due to diffidence and a culture of silence. One has to also accept the fact that women are also traditional and can also be conservative. Thus a Communist consciousness of equality does not come in a day. Women have to be economically independent and then only can they be free. In a feudal society like ours, development of a Communist consciousness will take time. Mukherjee stressed that we must remember that the main contradiction in our society is between classes and not between men and women. The women's struggle has to grow with the class struggle because there will be no success in the class struggle without women, nor will there be any success in the women's emancipation movement without class struggle.

Mukherjee traced the different phases through which the women's movement has traversed. "One must remember that prior to independence all the various streams of the independence movement—the Congress, the revolutionary parties, the Communists and others had one common goal—to defeat the imperialists and gain independence. In West Bengal, the Mahila Atma Raksha Samiti consisted initially of various ideologies, and many Communists, including myself, were in that organisation. After independence things changed. We broke away and became the Opposition, questioning the ruling Congress policies. Today the agitationist approach is less in West Bengal because we have a Left Front Government that is more responsive to our demands. Our voices are heard and there is no need to adopt an agitationist approach. The moment we raise an issue there is some response from the committees and some enquiry is made into the issue. There are also 17 women members in the Assembly and we have been able to make the government take some positive steps. The West Bengal Ganatantrik Mahila Samiti now has about 30 lakh members."

On the issue of Susheela Gopalan not being made the Chief Minister of Kerala[1] despite the media having projected her as the prospective Chief Minister during the election campaign, she was hesitant to respond, and only said, "I am unable to comment on that as I do not feel that they decided against her becoming CM just because she happened to be a woman."

Ahilya Rangnekar, also a member of the Central Committee of the CPI(M), has been involved with the party since the forties. She felt that her entry into politics was largely because of her upbringing and the progressive attitude of her father. The family atmosphere contributed in creating a lasting interest in politics. "My family, especially my father, was active in politics and so I grew up in an atmosphere where political issues were important. My father was a very progressive man and he decided to educate my sisters-in-law and me in spite of a great deal of social opposition. Despite considerable social pressure he remained firm in his decision. He encouraged me to always play games which boys did, and not to play with dolls. My brothers were also active in the trade union movement."

Rangnekar joined the students' movement in the thirties. She was sentenced to jail for six months during the Quit India Movement of 1942, a movement which, she stresses, was completely free of caste or religious bias. For the first time women came into politics, and it was observed that women were more militant than men. Rangnekar reminisces that, "there was a strong presence of Muslim women who fought along with us in the national movement, like Sophia Khan. It is these women who protested against the hierarchical treatment given to prisoners in terms of food, determined by

1 A Left Front Government came to power in Kerala after the 1996 elections.

their class and educational qualifications. Sophia Khan and Mrs Tyabji protested and insisted that all women will eat the same food. There was a sense of complete communal harmony."

Ahilya Rangnekar joined the party in 1943 and worked among textile workers. The relationship with the party, she pointed out, "did not hinder our own initiative in any way". She gives the example of the Parail (in Maharashtra) women's organisation which had a direct link with the party but also functioned with a separate agenda and raised issues such as price rise. "My party activities continued after my marriage as my husband was also a party member (1947)." She strongly feels that "in the post-independence period the attention given to women by political parties was less and they were often given weak seats by their party which they were bound to lose. I myself faced a problem in Parail in 1957 when, in spite of years of work in the constituency, I was not allowed to stand for the elections. But due to my political standing I was able to contest in the next elections and won from the constituency." She recognises the fact that Indian political history does show some positive trends for women—the right to vote was gained in 1934, some women like Vijayalaxmi Pandit rose to prominence—but even though small numbers of women continue to get elected to Assemblies and Parliament, overall, women's influence in politics has not increased.

After independence, whenever women tried to force a view that went against conventionally held notions about women and their rights within the family they faced tremendous opposition. During the Hindu Code Bill controversy in 1955-57, women in politics faced a great deal of abuse and harassment, especially in relation to the Anti-Bigamy Act. The arguments were at a very acrimonious level—for example, during the campaign women were told that "men had the right to marry seven times in order to have a male child". After 1977, Rangnekar feels, there has been a further decline in the willingness to accommodate women within the political system by all parties and hence the need for 33 per cent reservation. However, we have to be careful with reservation; it will increase visibiiity no doubt, but it can lead to exploitation and women being used as proxies for their husbands. But definitely with women entering the public arcna change is bound to come. The Panchayat elections have put forward 85 women in Thane district out of which 5 are *sarpanches,* for whom they are organising study circles with the aim of breaking the hold of their husbands. At the same time, contrary forces are working to restrict the impact of such efforts. For example, in Maharashtra due to a conservative government and the Shiv Sena dominance in local areas, we have found that attempts are being made to co-opt the women back into the domestic sphere. Pujas are being organised and women are called to participate, and through such activity the hold of tradition and the prescribed role for women is restored. So political parties have to make a concentrated effort to bring women out. Increasing communalisation has disrupted the mobilisation of women and divided the women's movement. But the positive aspect is that Muslim women have come out in the open demanding reform in the personal law and actively take part in demonstrations against communalism and oppression of women. They have protested against the right of the Muslim husband to divorce his wife by merely saying *Talaq talaq talaq'*.[2] However, there are also growing demands around religious lines that can lead to a certain breaking of the women's movement. Character assassination is a very common weapon used to pull women out of the movement."

On the question of the party's attitude to women and women's issues she said, "Our party has instructed that

2 Muslim Personal Law permits a man to divorce his wife by uttering these words in the presence of two male witnesses.

women's issues should be raised in all mass organisations.[3] There are fewer women in trade unions because there are limited women working in the factories as they are mainly involved in the packing industry and secretarial jobs. B. T. Ranadive of the CITU made a very conscious effort to bring women into trade unions by raising their problems."

"Women who rise in the party, are women who come up on political and individual merit only and relationships are not the determining factor. When women join the party they are taken to the grassroots level where they have to work, interact with people, understand the family and social structure. They also attend study circles and are taught how to carry out campaigns and relate to complex situations. From time to time we administer questionnaires in order to judge their level of understanding. I have never felt at a disadvantage being a woman in the party but I do feel at a disadvantage when I have to travel alone on the streets at night. I do believe that I have enjoyed a certain advantage because my husband and brother were both affiliated with the party; at least there was no opposition to my work."

She does not feel that there is a difference in the party's approach at the regional level. She explained, "The party follows a main policy and it applies at both the local and the national level. The party does support all women's issues in the local context but one has to understand that the situation is

3 Although in general women's issues are taken up by the AIDWA, they are also taken up by other frontal organisations of the party such as the CITU. Women workers under the banner of the CITU in mines, in the tobacco and *beedi* industries, in construction, plantations, etc., are fighting for their demands in joint campaigns of various trade union organisations. Under the guidance of the CITU, the All India Co-ordinating Committee of Working Women was founded in 1979 to tackle the specific problems of women that were neglected by trade unions such as equal wage for equal work, retrenchment, provision of crèches at the work place, and so on. Such wings or committees were formed at an international level in almost all countries to function along with trade unions. These wings raise specific problems relating to discrimination against women — wages, employment, promotion, sexual harassment, etc., as well as their promotion to higher bodies in trade unions.

different at the local level. Sometimes the situation is complex and we have to take stands according to the requirement. But there is a direct link between the party at the local and national levels."

> Women's issues are closely linked with the issues of education, poverty, wages, etc.

While speaking on the issue of Susheela Gopalan's candidature for Chief Ministership of Kerala, she said: "We all wanted her to be made CM, but Nayanar was more acceptable to all, and you must remember that since we have a coalition government in Kerala, we cannot force the issue. But if you notice, she has been given the Ministry of Industry which is today a difficult ministry and also moves away from the soft ministries which are usually given to women, like Women and Child Welfare."

She pointed to the discrimination women still continue to face in social life: "Women face a variety of discrimination and a major one is of guardianship of children. Women should be equal guardians for their children and their names should be equally valid for schools. In Maharashtra, we have conducted many independent campaigns relating to the issue of rape. One such was the Uttara case in which the man was sent to jail, but he is now out on bail. The legal system has its biases and delays. This case has been going on for 12 years without a firm decision. The man is allowed to go out on bail but the courts will not allow this young girl to marry. How long can she wait? She is 27 years old now."

Women's issues, according to Rangnekar, touch every aspect of life. In fact women's issues are closely linked with the issues of education, poverty, wages, etc. These issues have entered mainstream politics and no revolution is possible without women's issues being raised.

Susheela Gopalan is a member of the Central Committee of the CPI(M) and a popular figure in Kerala politics. She has emerged as a political figure of standing in Kerala with a considerable support base. After the 1996 Assembly elections she was tipped to be the next Chief Minister. However, the coalition government voted for Nayanar, a decision that generated quite a lot of speculation in the media. This became an issue also because the Left Parties profess a certain commitment to bringing women into mainstream politics. Added to this is the fact that Kerala has a high number of women voters and all parties had targeted women's issues to mobilise the women's vote.

Susheela Gopalan stressed the need for women's participation. She felt that involvement of women was a crucial factor in the development process and this included their participation in decision-making. "Women have to put pressure from within the party and they should be increasingly encouraged to join the party's mass organisations, the students' wing, trade unions, women's movement and the party. When the Communist movement started we had stressed the need for women to join the movement but as the movement grew this stress on women was lost."

Kerala has one of the largest number of women voters and in the recent elections women's issues dominated the manifestos of all parties, but in spite of this the number of women in actual politics is low. This, Gopalan feels, is due to the fact that in spite of high literacy, the social status of women has not actually changed. She says, "In Kerala literacy among women is high but working women on the whole are less. Among the upper classes there are a higher number of women working but among the working class the number is limited. In Kerala's rural economy, mainly commercial crops are grown where the work is done by men. Overall, the involvement of women in agricultural production is low. Women work primarily in the area of coir and cashew. In the beginning of the coir working-class movement the women had played an active role but they never rose to positions of leadership. Moreover, the middle-class concept of women staying at home if the man has a good job is also quite strong. At one point many areas in Kerala had a matrilineal system, where women had more control but even here all the affairs were managed by the maternal uncle and he controlled the women. Revolt against this system led to the adoption of the patriarchal system."

Gopalan stresses the need for women to come out into the public sphere. She says if women want a say in the decision-making process they must be involved in the process of social production. As both Marx and Lenin have said, it is only when women move out of the kitchen and participate equally in the production process, that they will be able to enjoy power in society. Employment of women is very important. In the domestic sphere women are isolated, and they must move out to the public sphere. The problem is that the woman's role as a mother, daughter is defined, but not as a citizen. Women and men are equal and women must have an equal say in the future of the country. We have to fight the prevalent thinking among men and women, both. Many women think of themselves as inferior to men and play a submissive role in the family. We have realised that it is only within a socialist means of production that women find space, and that is not possible in a competitive capitalist system.

Gopalan has changed her opinion on the issue of 33 per cent reservation keeping these things in mind. She says, "Initially I was against reservation but today there is no option. We have had some problems about selecting women to contest the municipal elections and the LDF committee cut down the number of women contesting the municipal elections. But now with Panchayat elections all parties have to cater to women and things are changing. When women become Panchayat members they acquire earning capacity and become ndependent. They acquire a certain respect and a status independent of their husbands. They develop confidence and can be trained as potential candidates for Assembly and

Parliamentary elections in the future."

"It is true that women in middle-class families are far more conservative and are often appointed in committees as show-pieces. The working-class women are far more aware as they face a daily struggle for survival. In Kerala we found that the middle-class women have to face a great deal of pressure from their families. We tried to find women to contest the elections but we realised that women do not have a base among men. Moreover, when you join politics you have to be prepared for family life to be disturbed, you have to go out and work among the people, in groups and in trade unions."

Personally, Gopalan has never faced discrimination in her political career nor did she feel disadvantaged. She looks back and says, "My first exposure to politics was at the age of 13 when I attended a coir workers' meeting which was addressed by my uncle. I was a rebel in college and had to change four colleges. I was very active in the students' movement. I stayed in Delhi for six years but eventually returned to Kerala and got involved in the trade union movement. Equal pay for equal work, maternity benefits, etc., were issues that had to be addressed not just through the women's movement but also through the trade unions. It is true that I had a lot of support from my family and my husband was a known party worker (A.K. Gopalan). I had the advantage of having no social and political pressures. I never faced discrimination and very soon I was elected to the District Committee and then the State Committee. I prepared a paper on how to develop the women's movement which was very well received. As a result I was one woman among 24 men in the Executive Committee. There were four of us in the State Council (women like Gowri Amma, Yasodhara, etc.).

Gopalan feels that her not becoming Chief Minister is a non-issue. She claimed she was never in the race. "I was never tipped for the post. In fact, I had not wanted to contest the elections at all and so I refused a ticket for the Lok Sabha polls. Finally, due to pressure I agreed to the Assembly elections. The media made an issue of my Chief Ministership, I did not want to be one at all. The controversy was that Nayanar was slated to be General Secretary and he was finally made Chief Minister. I was never in the picture. At present I am heading the Ministry of Industry. That is challenging and we are trying to revive the public sector undertakings. By controlling the Industry Ministry I can preserve the interests of women in traditional industries like *khadi* and handicrafts. Women are dominant in this area. Since I also control the Ministry of Social Welfare I will be able to effectively intervene in welfare programmes."

Brinda Karat, a young and dynamic Central Committee member, explained the organisational links between the AIDWA and the CPI(M). The AIDWA is an independent mass organisation of women, affiliated to the Left, but it is not a women's wing of the CPI(M). Many AIDWA members are CPI(M) party workers, but a large cross-section of women who join AIDWA do not necessarily have any party affiliation. The CPI(M) consists of party workers who are recruited directly. They can be working with the party on different fronts with organisations like the CITU, AIDWA, etc. "It is, however, true that AIDWA on the whole follows a Left ideology and we attract women to the Left."

"The AIDWA has today acquired a reputation of being the largest women's organisation in the country. A vast mass of women have joined AIDWA primarily due to the concentrated work of the organisation among women. The AIDWA has been active on all major issues relating to women and this has given it high visibility. In West Bengal this women's organisation has been very active, and as the party links are stronger there, it has been able to put a great deal of pressure on the government on issues related to women. The long campaign leading to the acceptance of the joint *patta* (joint ownership of land) is a clear example. West Bengal is the only State in the country where land reforms of such a nature have been passed. It is true that one's attitude of radical agitation does face a problem when one's own party is in power. But the Left women's organisations in West Bengal have definitely not became deputationists."

It is often misconstrued that Marxists believe that the women's struggle will start after the class struggle is over. They both have to happen together. The pressure by Communist women organisationally has forced the party to accept the increasing involvement of women in decision-making processes and to raise their problems. These debates are not publicly articulated because certain norms of inner party secrecy have to be maintained. Brinda claimed that party documents reveal that the party has been self-critical and called for rectification of feudal attitudes towards women prevailing in certain sections of the party and the movements it leads. However, she was quick to point out that debate within the party on these issues are not publicly articulated because of certain essential norms of communist functioning.

West Bengal

In West Bengal the CPI(M), alongwith its other Left Front allies, has been in power for the last two decades. We find that the Left and the Congress both enjoy 35-40 per cent of popular support, while the remaining 10 per cent vacillates and determines the winning party. The support for the CPI(M) is far more in the rural areas while the Congress is popular in the cities. Calcutta is no longer a Left bastion because of the disillusionment of the middle class whose aspirations have not been fulfilled. Caste and religious divisions do not play as important a role in electoral politics here as they do in other parts of the country.

The popularity of the Left has been attributed largely to the agrarian reforms brought about by the government. Historically, Bengal has been characterised by early reform movements specifically directed towards the emancipation of women. The dominance of Left politics has not hindered, even if we assume that it has not encouraged, the women's movement or questioned the importance of women's emancipation. Consequently, awareness of social issues and a desire for women's emancipation is higher here than in most other States. Despite this we find that politics continues to be short of women: there are only 21 women out of 291 members in the Vidhan Sabha of which 17 belong to the CPI(M).

The political history of the CPI(M) governments in power is not devoid of controversies around women's issues. A controversy had originated around the CPI(M) role in two incidents, the Bantala and the Birati rape cases. In the Bantala event, Anita Dewanji, a health worker travelling with two officers, was attacked near Bantala village and killed. The second instance was when five women living in the Birati slum were raped. Both these crimes were said to have been perpetrated by hooligans affiliated with the CPI(M). Both these areas are strong CPI(M) strongholds and though there was no immediate or direct involvement of the party, the party was accused of taking a passive line. The situation was further complicated by some women CPI(M) members taking a stand that the women who were raped were of dubious character. One of the raped women was accused of having links with the liquor mafia. This situation placed the AIDWA in a precarious position between party politics and women's issues. They had to tread the middle path of retaining their individual agenda of protecting women's issues even while not being disloyal to the party. But it is evident that it was pressure from the AIDWA and the PBGMS that made the government take action against the criminals in these as well as other incidents.

In spite of a controversial statement by the PBGMS leader Shyamali Gupta that talked about the loose character of these women, the organisation itself mounted pressure to get relief for the women and to arrest the criminals. However, it does not appear to have had the kind of force and militancy evident in the AIDWA campaigns on national issues like *sati*, Shah Bano, etc. The Left Party being part of the government made the PBGMS tone down its opposition to the government and negotiation rather than confrontation seemed to be the norm. However, it is quite evident that the PBGMS has never been reduced to a deputationist organisation like the Mahila Congress in Madhya Pradesh.

Jasodhara Bagchi, woman activist and Head of the Department of Women's Studies at Jadavpur University, felt that "due to the pressure of the women's movement, there was a conviction in the Bantala case. Although not the perpetrators of the crime, the Left were defensive. In the Birati case we found that the issue was turned into one of women with easy virtue, and it was a line of defence used by the party. It is important in these situations for the women in the party to always be alert and question these kind of biases which often justify injustices in society."

On the issue of women's political participation Bagchi felt that, "the Left Parties are congenial to women entering politics but how much effort they will make is debatable. In fact it is this ambiguity which makes NGOs a little wary of aligning with political parties. But we do align on certain women's issues as it is important to have a mass support and be able to put pressure on the government. The CPI(M) does have women who have been involved in movements earlier so there is a tradition of women's participation." She also feels that there is today greater space in the party ideology for women. Many of them have also come up from the grassroot level. Even when middle-class women join the CPI(M), they have to work at the grassroot level in order to rise in the party. Women like Sudha Rai and Mahashweta Devi have been involved with the tribal and workers' movements for a long time and their identity is far more important now than that of middle-class feminists.

Bagchi raises the problem of discourse that often traps the very people who think they can use it to their advantage. She mentions how this has been a problem with the CPI(M): "It has continuously made reference to and used familial language like *Maa, Bau*. These words carry with them images and relationships that eventually put women into subservient positions even in the political arena. Somehow it forces a woman to adapt to this respectable image, although I can understand why it is used as in a mass movement it helps to forge links and build up empathy. The legacy of cultural nationalism is a millstone around the neck of women. In fact the growth of the BJP has at least made us conscious of the dangers of this ideology. Another important fact is that all projects for development like family planning are targeted at only women. The CPI(M) has at times also adopted the attitude that the women's movement interferes with and divides the working-class movement. This thinking has started to change in the last few years, but it will take time."

Although Bagchi gave unequivocal support for the 33 per cent reservation for women in the Panchayati Raj institutions, in relation to reservation in Assemblies and Parliament she says, "The need is that women should demand a share in the power rather than reservation, it may not ensure sharing of power."

Kumkum Chakravarty, a bank employee and Vidhan Sabha member, has been in politics since her student days. She felt that the greatest hindrance to women entering and rising in politics is our society itself. It not only prevents them from entering active politics but once in politics it also makes them hesitant. According to Chakravarty, her party always raises protest against any sort of atrocity perpetrated on women and their social problems. The very ideology of the party is emancipation of mankind which includes emancipation of both men and women. Hence it matters little that in the State Committee of the party, for instance, the number of women representatives is less. She went on to say: "It is important for us women to fight and be heard and pressurise the party into accepting our point of view. It is easier for us urban educated women to stand up for our rights but often the poor rural woman does get oppressed. But as women we do keep up the pressure on the government."

"But we have to realise that when we fight Vidhan Sabha elections we have to deal with all aspects of the people's problems and cater to the community as a whole. So no election can be fought on only women's issues." But it is equally true that when a woman comes to her with a problem she gives them special attention. Women can at times understand the pressures of another woman better. In fact for her the biggest lacuna in the party structure is that a woman can only approach the PBGMS with their problems. "A destitute woman is basically the responsibility of all democratic institutions and not just women's organisations. Thus we have ended up isolating women into a separate category."

Chakravarty feels reservation in Panchayats has made a difference and "we have discovered that with reservation more women are coming into politics. The party has organised training programmes so as to develop their greater understanding about politics."

Shyamali Gupta, a member of the PBGMS and an active party worker, felt that the AIDWA has had a positive impact on the party. "The AIDWA has brought about some change in the party attitude. The West Bengal Ganatantrik Mahila Samiti was formed in 1943 and the AIDWA was born out of it in 1980. I have been associated with the AIDWA since its very inception. I was a member of the Ganatantrik Samiti from 1963 and we were involved in the price rise, land reform, Tebhaga and *Nari Mukti* movements. But women's emancipation will take a long time, we have to have women in all movements, for education, democratic rights and land rights. There has to be a demand in all sectors for women's emancipation and equality."

"The emergence of the AIDWA has enabled women to formulate and articulate their own set of demands. The AIDWA has kept up the pressure on the government by submitting its list of demands. These demands include: (1) compulsory marriage registration; (2) joint *patta* holdings and the conversion of all single *patta* to joint *patta*; (3) family courts in all districts; (4) identity cards; and (5) minimum wages for women working in the unorganised sector. The government has already started the process for joint *patta* and about 3 lakh joint *pattas* have been already registered. The government is carrying out the process of converting all single holdings allotted in the last 10 years to joint *patta*."

On the question of women's participation and sharing of power, Gupta felt that the party should pay more attention. Out of 82 members in the State Committee, only 7 are women. There is no woman in the Politburo and only 5 in the Central Committee. "The problem is that our party members are sometimes feudal. In theory the party ideology provides space for women's empowerment but in practice there is opposition to it. I feel that women are given seats where the party's position is weak, so the women are bound to lose. Looking back, however, there has been an improvement. In 1982 there were no women but at least now there are some women. So the change is for the better."

She also feels that men by and large do not want reservation for women and are now trying to stall it by trying to bargain with the numbers. She says, "We do find that the men are resenting 33 per cent reservation and feel that 25 per cent is enough. I would also like to add that the whole party does not always react positively on women's issues and in the context of sharing power the situation becomes even more complex."

So the real problem is "the attitude of the men. Most men are used to dealing with male colleagues, they find it difficult to relate to women. Women on the other hand are often not assertive and readily accept male domination. The emancipation of women is closely linked with the gender sensitisation of men. The other problem we face is that when the issue is from outside the party, the men respond positively, but they are not so responsive about women when it comes to internal party politics. But the party leadership is making an effort as was evident in the *Panchayat* elections. The attitude of the women has to also change, they have to realise their rights, be aware of political situations and educate themselves."

On the question of unity with other political groups: "It becomes at times difficult to work together with other women's groups because of ideological differences." In West Bengal, "women as a whole can never work as a pressure group because the ideologies of the Congress and the Left Front combine are very different. Women cannot be made to unite across ideologies. Politically also it becomes difficult as the CPI(M) and the Congress are rivals in West Bengal. We are working in collaboration with other women's organisations but not the AIWC."

Chhaya Beda, Minister of State for Employment Generation, and an active AIDWA and party worker, feels that the main reason that women are left behind is that, "women are not educated enough and so they are not able to come forward. There is no special programme initiated by the party to encourage women. In the old days many women came through participation in movements; when I was a student I joined the movement for education during the fifties and sixties. I later joined the teachers' movement and now I am in politics." There are still very few women in organisational positions in the party. This, according to Beda, is because women are hindered by factors such as late nights, and the pressure of domestic work. A woman today carries the double burden of maintaining the family and carrying on one's career. She says, "My family was always anti-Congress and although my husband was a government employee he never stopped me."

If we make an effort, Beda feels, "we can mobilise women. It is a definite fact that women do come out when we call them to meetings and address their problems. Reservation in Panchayat has generated a greater desire in women to participate. Today the party is making efforts to make women participate. But the party rules for recruitment remain just as rigid. There are party rules that require that we first observe each individual woman and then only on the basis of output we make the woman a party member. The AIDWA is a mass organisation so it is easy to become a member, but the party is different, one has to prove ones credibility in order to be a party member. The party does not randomly pick up members. This kind of procedure limits the ability of the party to recruit a large number of women into the party."

For Beda, reservation is important today because women have not entered politics or have not been able to enter politics in the normal course, although she personally has never felt a hindrance in being a woman. She felt women were increasingly occupying positions of importance, and gave the example of four Ministers in the Left Front Government today, stressing the fact that these women were controlling important portfolios, like Family Welfare, Forests, Mass Education, and Employment Generation.

Malini Bhattacharya is an active party member and was twice elected MP from the Jadavpur parliamentary constituency.[4] She joined the CPI(M) in 1975 after a few years of deliberation. In the 1960s and 70s there was a democratic movement in West Bengal led by the Left Front and the Centre was hostile to the Left. At that stage she and her husband decided that they must be affiliated with the movement. Her years in England also helped her to attend study circles and understand the Marxist ideology. Initially, she was involved with teachers and the cultural movement.

In 1989, the party decided that she should contest the elections, which she won against Mamata Banerji from the Jadavpur constituency. She was accused by some women's

4 She however lost the 1996 elections in the face of an anti-CPI(M) wave in Calcutta. She lost to Krishna Bose of the Congress and Malini Bhattacharya's defeat was considered one of the major upsets of the West Bengal elections in 1996.

groups of fighting another woman but then she says, "I realised that I also represented an ideology and was fighting against the Congress brand of politics. So I went ahead and won the seat. Then in 1991 Mamata Banerji shifted to South Calcutta and I once again won the seat."

She regrets the fact there are only six per cent women in the party. "I feel that there are many women workers in the mass organisations who should be incorporated into the party. But women have to be more assertive in the party." She says she has found that if a woman asserts herself then she is recognised and she is heard. They have to prove their worth as committed party workers. She has sometimes found that the women's organisation associated with the party in West Bengal depends on the party infrastructure to organise their activities (be it a seminar, conference or demonstration). If women can prove that they can work and take responsibility on their own they will definitely be heard. But if they continue to be dependent they will never really be taken seriously.

One problem is that there are few women in the party. Generally, she says, "I do sometimes find that the male comrades do not have a sense of equality when they relate to women comrades. But we must remember that when we join the party we all carry with us our own cultural and ideological thinking of which feudalism and patriarchy are very much a part. Consequently, it is only through a process of political education that both men and women can learn that principle of equality which is an essential component of socialist thinking. The experience of the *Panchayat* elections has been educational, as many of the women who won were not even party members. Now there should be an attempt to bring some of these women into the mass organisation and the party. In West Bengal we generally find that if a man is a member then his wife is also a sympathiser. But there are also many situations when we have women who are members of PBGMS and the men are affiliated with the Congress. This does lead to friction in the domestic sphere, which I think is inevitable."

The PBGMS is working towards sensitising women to become conscious of their rights and encouraging them to join the party. In fact in the urban areas there has been some change in the man-woman relationship and we find that the domestic work is being shared. In the rural areas too some change is perceptible especially after the Panchayat elections. She says, "It has led to new tensions that are positive for the woman."

Looking at the evolution of the left women's movement, Bhattacharya feels that during the seventies a lid seemed to have been put on all democratic and human rights movements. The imposition of Emergency by Mrs. Gandhi, the then Prime Minister, was one manifestation of this. "The upsurge of struggle that followed brought many women into the left movement. The declaration of the International Decade of Women gave a new impetus to the women's movement and new organisations were generated. But the political component in PBGMS's thinking set it apart from other women's organisations. There has been a change from that situation today, with AIDWA, while keeping its political belief intact, making a conscious effort to align with other left women's organisation and NGOs. There is an effort for joint programmes due to the realisation that effective measures can only be ensured by larger mobilisation of women and unity over certain common issues. However, there may be situations like in West Bengal, where we may have basic problems with the ideological stand of the Mahila Congress and the Mahila BJP; as a result, no alliance is possible."

"The AIDWA has not become deputationist even though we have a left government in power in the state. But there is a definite difference between our approach to the Central Government, and a Left Front State Government. Controversies are much less here as we feel that demands raised by the women's organisations are being looked into by the government. We also feel that the movement against price rise, unemployment and the new economic policy should be mainly addressed to the Central Government as these are their responsibility. In the early years of the Left Front Government it was very important that we should focus on the democratisation of the Centre-State relationship. The Left Government encouraged all these democratic movements but movements against dowry and atrocities took a back seat for some years. The attempt now is to focus on women's issues that had gone unattended. The AIDWA is now making attempts to restore the focus on women with the joint *patta* system by which the woman, in case of a break in the family, will not be left destitute, she will be a joint owner of the land. They are trying to introduce the idea of compulsory registration of marriages but are facing some opposition from some sections both within and outside the party."

Bhattacharya concludes that, "the ideology of the Left Party does give space to women to participate in politics. A part of the battle for space has already been fought for us by the earlier CC members, so we have to now struggle to acquire a stronger voice within the party. The party is at that stage when it has accepted the need to mobilise women, to have women in the party, but it is now important to make sure that these policies are implemented. Take, for example, the decision for the allotment of more tickets in Parliament and Assemblies made at the State Committee level and approved by the Central Committee. There has been an attempt to bring more women into electoral politics but the situation is still not very encouraging. There are only two women elected to Parliament and 17 Vidhan Sabha members."

Anil Biswas of the CPI(M) is an active party worker and member of the State Committee. He agreed that women should be part of the government and it was a weakness that women have not been given opportunities. "But the situation is improving. The party has 20,000 women in its two lakh party membership. The role of women during the Panchayat elections has been particularly inspiring. We have increased our efforts for providing training programmes for the women who have been elected into Panchayats. But the problem is that all this will take time as women first have to be uplifted from economic deprivation and then only we can deal with political and ideological training. We must remember that we cannot impose ideology and the attempt has to be to change women's attitude."

Biswas would have us believe that the onus of the lack of political participation of women is on women themselves—"their attitudes". Such a simplistic understanding of such a complex issue came as a great surprise to us especially after the sensitive and insightful comments of the Communist women.

The Emergence of Regional Parties 8

The Lok Sabha elections of 1996 have brought about a major change in the nature of Indian politics. For the first time we saw the emergence of regional political parties with strong caste and community affiliations. These parties essentially locate their support base in a particular region or community and are primarily created to address their grievances. They have today become a voice for many marginalised and oppressed sections of Indian society and have changed the very complexion of Indian politics. The Samajwadi Party (SP) and Bahujan Samaj Party (BSP) (in Uttar Pradesh and some presence in other states as well), Telugu Desam (TDP) (in Andhra Pradesh), Tamil Manila Congress (TMC) and Dravida Munnetra Kazagham (DMK) (in Tamil Nadu) are some of the regional parties that have come together under the banner of the United Front Government. They are said to represent the forces of secularism and the voice of oppressed sections.

The primary reasons for the emergence of these parties in north India have been the growing consciousness among the backward and Scheduled Castes/Tribes in States like Uttar Pradesh that the national parties (primarily the Congress and the BJP) do not represent their interests, as they are dominated by the upper castes, in conjunction with a decline of national parties like the Congress. This dissatisfaction manifested itself in terms of the rise of such parties as the Samajwadi Party and the Bahujan Samaj Party. Although the BJP has been able to show considerable success in electoral terms in these regions by winning a large number of seats, this has taken the form of consolidation of upper-caste votes rather than mobilisation of the backward and deprived sections.

Samajwadi Party (Uttar Pradesh)

The States of northern India have generally been economically backward and socially dominated by feudal and caste relations. The Mandal[1] factor and the division of political vote-banks around caste have been a marked development of recent years. The main force uniting the United Front that represents the third force (the Janata Dal-Left Front -Samajwadi Party alliance), who actively supported the Mandal Report, is the caste factor, and its calculations of electoral success have been based on alliances of different backward communities. Of late, religion too has become an important factor in the scheme of things because of the rise of the Right-wing BJP, specially after the demolition of the Babri Masjid in Ayodhya. The result was the alienation of the Muslims from the Congress, who they felt had let them down on the issue of the Masjid, and increased support for the Samajwadi Party and other secular parties of the United Front.

Thus the game of political numbers in the last election (1996) gave birth to three broad coalitions, the BJP and the Samata Party, the Congress and the Bahujan Samaj Party and the United Front or Third Front. All these coalitions staked their victories on a calculation of various caste and religion-based vote-banks.

Caste-based politics has always been equated with casteism, and has therefore been considered to be retrograde and divisive. The assumption has been that caste-based politics represent semi-feudal relations and alliances based on caste allow no space either for progressive politics or for more equitable gender

[1] The Mandal Commission was set up by the Congress Government to look into the issue of reservation for Other Backward Castes (OBCs) in colleges and government jobs. However, after the report was submitted it merely gathered dust for many years because the Congress feared the impact of the report on various vote-banks. The Opposition had pressed for the tabling of the report. When the Janata Government came to power under Prime Minister V.P. Singh, the report was tabled. There was widespread agitation against the report that ultimately led to the fall of the government. Later, however, during the next Congress Government's rule, the report was accepted without so much as a whimper.

relations. It has also been assumed that regional parties lack a wider vision on issues of gender due to the greater pressures of local conservatism. After all, it is in response to local needs and aspirations that these parties have emerged and they have come to be closely linked to regional cultural identities and regional pride. On the other hand, it also brings into the power game a different class of political elite, a non-English speaking, non-Westernised, *desi* (native) elite, whom the city-bred, Westernised, even progressive intelligentsia identify with a lack of culture (defined in terms of the progressive Western variety), crudeness, and cultural and political conservatism. If we are to accept this analysis of the present political scenario, especially in north India, given the configuration of political and economic backwardness coexisting with caste and communal politics, it is indeed a grim picture.

At the same time, the political pundits inform us that we are now in an era of coalition politics. Does this mean a step backward for the women's movement? How do the regional parties respond to the pressure for the increasing participation of women in politics? We would like to examine the situation in Uttar Pradesh[2] and the Samajwadi Party, to understand these emerging trends. In Uttar Pradesh, the Samajwadi Party, with the largest support base in the Third Front, has emerged as a strong force against the BJP with a dual agenda of secularism and upliftment of the lower castes. It has consolidated its vote among the Muslims and the lower castes, and is making an effort to mobilise the farmers, as is clear by its alliance with Ajit Singh's group. The alliance with Ajit Singh was also an attempt to bring back the Jat votes that the Third Front had lost in the wake of the Mandal agitation.

Since the entire game-plan of elections is based on vote calculations, who can garner the votes of which sections, becomes a determining factor in the allocation of seats. Caste

[2] One of the northern States of India, located in the Gangetic plain, which has one of the largest populations.

played a major role in the choice of women candidates in the 1996 elections.

In OBC-Dalit dominated Mirzapur, for instance, the Samajwadi Party fielded the "Bandit Queen", Phoolan Devi of Nishad (dalit) caste, against the upper-caste candidate, Thakur Virendar Singh of the BJP. Her candidature sharply polarised votes in the constituency, almost exclusively on the basis of caste. It is interesting to note how the tragedy of Phoolan's life was turned to major political advantage during the lead-up to the elections. Phoolan's life became an example of the oppression and sexual exploitation which poor lower-caste women almost routinely face; she became a symbol of rebellion against these caste-based injustices. In the course of her campaign, Phoolan herself sought to make these connections with women voters.

Her responses to questions addressed to her in an interview are telling:

> *Q. Women seem to be quite influenced by you, are you depending on them for your electoral prospects?*
>
> A. They all are confident that I will protect them from humiliation and oppression.
>
> *Q. Do you think the law should be changed for checking growing incidents of women's rape?*
>
> A. Of course, I will raise this issue in Parliament—laws should be amended, giving stern punishment to rapists. Usually they manage to go scot-free as women are too shy to speak about it in the courts. There should be separate women courts besides women police stations.

The support for Phoolan from women was also polarised along caste lines. There seemed to be no recognition of the fact that gender cuts across caste lines and that oppression within castes of women is quite as bad. In fact, women proved to be the crucial weapon in the campaign for both parties. Phoolan's opponents, the *thakurs*, tried to use the women of their community to counter her. Attempts were made by the BJP to organise a *Vidhwa Yatra* (a procession of widows) from Behmai village, of the 22 Rajput widows whose husbands had allegedly been killed by Phoolan Devi in 1981. Although subsequently banned by the courts, the objective of this procession was to win the sympathy of the electorate. "With the prayer for their dear-departed on their lips, the poor widows of this village performed *'aartis'* at the martyrs' memorial before clambering on to their *Vidhwa Rath* to embark on a 'journey in quest of justice'. Tears streaking down their faces and their voices choked with emotion, the widows bade goodbye to the village-folk, who accorded them a warm send-off amidst shouts of *'hame insaaf chahiye'* ('we want justice') and full-throated calls to all Kshatriyas to teach Phoolan, the killer, a lesson through the ballot."[3] Munni Devi, who was allegedly widowed by Phoolan Devi's bullets when she was only eleven years old, reiterated her vow that she would not rest till Phoolan is hanged. "I want justice . . . why are the police after us? Why is our *rath* stopped while the *raths* of others are allowed?" she wailed. Unfortunately, nobody felt the need to raise the issue that Munni Devi, in spite of having become a widow at 11 had not remarried. It is, of course, quite obvious that the full-throated cries for revenge could as well be directed by the widows at the society that have kept them widows for more than a decade after the Behmai massacre, even if the allegations against Phoolan Devi turned out to be true.

For the lower castes, Kanshi Ram and Mayavati may be their political voices, but their avenging angel is Phoolan Devi. Common to all these constructions of the image of Phoolan is the image of challenge to authority, whether social or governmental, which is perceived as an effort to subvert a system that is inadequate, insensitive and incapable of giving them a fair deal. A direct corollary is the sudden concern over the criminalisation of politics on the part of the state and the

3 *The Pioneer*, 29 April 1996.

elite. It is now common to hear remarks like: "How will the country's progressive people take to people like this (referring to Phoolan) sitting in Parliament?" (a woman politician and now senior journalist).

Our respected politicians are known to have been using criminals for their own ends since the early years of our independence. Further, the question of who is a criminal has become more complex with the revelations of the various scams. But perhaps a 'cultured' criminal is more acceptable than crude marginals who become criminals in order to stand up to a system that humiliates and oppresses them at every stage. This is not to romanticise crime but to point out that in a social system that does not allow a poor *harijan* to even stand with self-respect before the upper castes, how are they going to compete for political power? Every act of rebellion or retribution therefore becomes a criminal act—force is used to achieve that which cannot be achieved peacefully within the present structure of power.

Phoolan Devi is a phenomenon that cannot be easily explained. A poor Scheduled Caste village woman subjected to repeated rape suddenly transforms herself into an avenging *Kali* to give her tormentors from an upper-caste male-dominated society a taste of their own medicine—the tormentors were, according to her own confession, castrated and the myth of upper-class superiority shredded through bullets. This might sound like scenes from a B-grade movie, but if reports are to be believed, the Scheduled Castes, irrespective of sex, thronged the streets to have a glimpse of the woman who had broken down the centuries-old wall of abject surrender to reassert her rights. The votes were not for Phoolan Devi *per se* but for her bullets that symbolised justice in a society where the "law" was but an instrument of subjugation.

The very success ratio of these 'new leaders' whose bullets have won for them popular ballots is an effect

> not a cause. Above everything else, it symbolises the changing polity of India and the growing contradictions between politics and a political structure that is deemed inadequate to match aspirations. The people's mandate for these people is not for them to go and plead their cause and represent them in the precincts of Parliament. It is for them to assert and grab their rights and dignity—the ballot has consciously chosen the bullet as its symbol. The message is clear: it is high time there is a serious debate on the necessity of matching polity with politics.[4]

She understands the rules of the game and is ready to bend them to serve her purpose. She is honest to her cause— upliftment of the lower castes, and is capable of inspiring people to believe in it. Phoolan Devi is one woman who has a desire to fight for her rights. She is known to have said in her campaign speeches, "I may be considered illiterate by the BJP, but life has educated me in ways which most people would not have faced. I have learnt from the bullets of the police, the oppression of the upper-caste and ultimately that of being a woman." What is most inspiring about Phoolan is her desire to convert the atrocities faced by her into weapons to fight oppression, without taking refuge under the image of a victim. In fact for most villagers, especially women, she is the image of *Durga*. She constantly asserts this aggressive militant aspect of her personality. She says, "Women are equal to men and as a woman I feel that I can do as well as a man in politics. In fact women are better as they are more courageous, more conscious and less corrupt. I strongly feel that there should be 50 per cent reservation for women. Women today have difficult battles to fight such as the atrocity of child marriage. In my own life I have faced severe oppression as a little girl, in the way I spoke, dressed and other habits. But one has to fight."

4 *The Hindustan Times*, 2 June 1996

Despite this fiery image of a rebel and an outcaste who encourages the underprivileged to rebel against their oppression, ironically enough, in reality Phoolan's lifestyle is taking on the shades of middle-class living, and she is, consciously or unconsciously, making attempts to conform to accepted notions of respectability. Her appeal to large sections of the masses is in terms of their ability to identify with her, she may well lose that advantage if she changes too much too fast. These contradictions will take time to be resolved, as Phoolan Devi is also a reflection of the contradictions in the Samajwadi Party. While the SP has a large support base, it has failed to consolidate it except along lines of caste and religion and it continues to rely largely on the support of the Yadavs and the Muslims. In the complicated structure of caste hierarchies even the Yadavs are known to be caste oppressors at a certain level, and have in fact gained further advantage because of their alliance with Mulayam Singh Yadav. Although Phoolan sees the need for a wider political perspective in her repeated references to development, education, and the need to change people's lives, her party, with its heavy involvement in electoral politics, is not able to provide that perspective. The SP's main achievement lies in its success in creating effective alternative pressure groups that represent other than established interests.

The Assembly Elections of 1996 reinforced the trends that became evident in the Lok Sabha polls, with its own unique flavour of local political history and constraints. Caste politics, hostility to women candidates, and religious biases were far more evident. There was a nominal increase in the number of tickets given to women—as against 107 women candidates in 1993, 188 women were in the fray in 1996, with the BJP fielding 27, the BSP 10, the Samajwadi Party 17, and the rest being mostly independents.[5] Our interviews

[5] *Northern India Patrika*, 25 September 1996.

and discussions revealed that women faced the same marginalising experience in ticket allotment as at the national level. Given constraints of time and space we were able to investigate only the Maharajganj and Gorakhpur areas, which have certain characteristic as well as unique features. For the 45 Assembly seats in the area, the BJP had put up one women candidate, the BSP none and the Samajwadi Party 5 (in alliance with JD).

Great chaos and confusion prevailed in all parties over ticket allotment at the State level. The SP had its own share of confusion which, according to party workers, was because of a lack of organisational structure. All power seemed to be centred in one man, the former Chief Minister, Mulayam Singh Yadav. Hence accessibility to him was important for any potential candidate. This was compounded by the fact that the SP is not well knit organisationally, and its actions are often based on spontaneous reactions. However, admiration for the leadership of Mulayam Singh Yadav was evident among most Samajwadi women; they felt he was trying to give an impetus to women's political participation, as the SP had given four seats to women in the Gorakhpur/Maharajganj area. According to them, unlike the BJP and the BSP, the SP has understood the political importance of the women's vote and so it went ahead with 33 per cent reservation in Panchayat elections. Most voters felt that Mulayam Singh had the necessary vision, but he was not being able to elevate the party from the level of petty politics due to lack of decentralisation and poor party infrastructure.

The confusion in ticket allotment was further compounded by the alliance with JD, and controversies over seat adjustments. Many disgruntled candidates found out at the last minute, that they had lost their tickets to JD candidates. Women were the great sufferers in these situations, since they were hastily displaced to accommodate 'winning' male candidates, as happened in Panyira Assembly constituency in Maharajganj.

A social worker **Talat Aziz** had filed her candidature on an SP ticket only to find that the seat had been given to JD in the alliance. With the people's support and her own initiative, she finally forced the SP to restore her as the official candidate. However, again two days before the election at the Prime Minister's election meeting, it was announced that the JD candidate was the official UF candidate, with the result that Talat Aziz had to withdraw at the last moment. The United Front lost the seat and it also affected the results in neighbouring constituencies.

The Janata Dal had first intended to field **Manju Zakki** from this constituency, but because of the pressure of their high command her candidature was shifted to Gorakhpur city, known to be a BJP stronghold with a large RSS support base. The chances of Zakki's winning this seat were very low. Both Talat Aziz and Manju Zakki complained of hostility from the party leaders; they felt they had eventually got the tickets due to their own initiative, education, social status and party political contacts. Manju Zakki said, "I have a certain position and so I have access, but many grassroot workers who have done so much of work and have struggled do not get party tickets. The mental calibre of political parties is so low that they treat women as objects. The leaders want around themselves women who can entertain them. Political parties do not encourage women who have a mind of their own and can enter into debates and contest on an equal basis. The hostility to women exists right from the main party leadership down to the lower local levels. The leadership has no place for women who are activists, women who are strong and who cannot be controlled. The struggle for women to acquire recognition in the party is a long one. Even if the 33 per cent Reservation Bill is passed, men will not easily hand over power to women. The problem exists in the whole party organisation that is not ready to accept women. The party at the national level may seem very liberal but they will not support you in case of a controversy over a ticket. Even national level leaders like Deve Gowda, Paswan and Sharad Yadav will only give women place in committees if they have to accommodate a Dalit woman. They are not giving us a chance to come up, how do they expect to encourage women from the grassroots level? I myself have been eventually given a weak seat in Gorakhpur that is known to be a BJP stronghold. In case I fail to win, I will be blamed as a woman."

Talat Aziz asserted that the main problems arose because of the lack of organisational infrastructure in the party. She felt that biases against women were strong at lower levels in the party structure and that no real attempt had been made to gender sensitise the men of the party. She recalls, "As a member of the committee to select candidates for the parliamentary elections I have often found that men are chauvinistic with very little sympathy for women." At the same time, she also observed that "during my experience as vice-president of the women's wing of the SP, I have found that more than 80 per cent of the women do not take politics seriously. The women's wing primarily functioned from Lucknow."

"There are two kinds of women who joined the women's wing. One belonging to influential families who manipulate and get their work done (these women were primarily engaged in providing people help in acquiring admission facilities and health requirements). They hardly participated in any grassroot-level activity. The other group of women were rural woman who were selected on the basis of their caste and community. These women had strong ties within the community. There are very few women who have risen to the Assembly level through their own efforts. The efforts of women like Phoolan Devi, Sharda Devi, Gauri Devi are admirable. They may have used caste as an initial stepping-stone, but they have been able to consolidate their position through their own personal commitment and energy." Talat further points out, "one must remember that for a woman to come out from the home, the support of her family is very important. I may be lucky in this respect but in general women are oppressed and find it difficult to venture into politics." According to her, the tragedy is that in this area there is no women's movement, nor have the circumstances been created for the development of one. The basic issues of *'Rozi Roti, Kapda aur Makan'* (food, clothing and housing) are still very relevant. An important point that Talat Aziz made was that caste, community and family affiliations still dominated over gender considerations.

Gauri Devi initially won the Assembly elections because of a sympathy vote (after the violent death of her husband). Since then she has been able to form a strong base for herself. She has won the Assembly seat of Koduja thrice and was contesting for the fourth time in 1996. Brought into politics by the violent death of her husband Ravindar Singh, a popular student leader, over time she has acquired a popularity of her own. The main reason for her popularity is her accessibility to the people; despite being Rajput (upper-caste Hindu) she has been able to mobilise the support of the Nishads, and Muslims.

Sharda Devi (Mundera Assembly constituency) joined politics on her own and has contested the Vidhan Sabha seat thrice. Her family was connected with the Chauri Chaura[6] incident during the period of the independence movement. Her political ambitions centred around doing something for her area. She said: "I am primarily concerned with getting development work done in my area, getting schools, roads and medical centres set up. I strongly feel that I have a right to be a Minister and intend to fight for it if I win the elections. I feel that I have lost out on this opportunity previously because of the changes that occurred due to my

[6] The Chauri Chaura massacre took place during the freedom struggle when a large group of villagers burnt a police thana burning alive a number of policemen. Gandhi temporarily withdrew his agitation fearing both retaliation and loss of the non-violent character of his movement.

changing party affiliations — first the Janata Party, then the Lok Dal and now SP. But I have never felt at a disadvantage as a woman."

The party sought to capitalise on Phoolan Devi's popularity by giving a ticket to her husband from the Pipraich constituency. The calculation was that she would be able to influence Nishad votes in adjacent constituencies as well. Many of the other women candidates were counting on her for support. But she was greatly disturbed and was willing to take on even Mulayam Singh Yadav for trapping her to campaign in a constituency where the other candidate (BJP) was also a Nishad. She did not want the fight to be between two Nishads, giving evidence to the fact that her caste affiliations were much stronger than her political affiliation. But she is, at the same time, smart enough to recognise the importance of party politics in a democracy. Umed Singh did contest on a Samajwadi ticket from Pipraich. But despite Phoolan's best efforts and her unmistakeable popularity, he lost to the BJP candidate. Phoolan had correctly understood the implications of a divided community on electoral politics.

The other two women candidates of the Samajwadi Party were **Prabhawati Rawat** and **Shubhawati Devi** both of whom canvassed for sympathy votes. They belong to the Dalit community and have the backing of their community. Shubhawati Devi is the wife of a self-styled Robin Hood, Om Prakash Paswan, who had enjoyed a great deal of power and credibility among the local people. However, in spite of being part of an election campaign and winning a Lok Sabha election in 1996, she has shown no development in political consciousness.[7] She said: "I campaigned by just appealing to the people with folded hands, I did not even need to give a speech. I just silently requested them to help me in getting

[7] However, Sharda Devi did assert that she was interacting with the Panchayat members in her area and was trying to raise their political consciousness through training programmes.

justice for the murder of my husband." She contested and won the Assembly seat, after which she vacated the Parliamentary seat for her son.

All the women of the SP interviewed felt that reservation was a necessity, if women were to take active part in politics. Many did feel that after the present Panchayat elections most of the women pradhans were being controlled by their husbands, but they also felt that over time the situation will remedy itself. The women interviewed themselves are clear examples of the fact – they have moved out of the domestic sphere and will eventually start asserting the power they have acquired, although the tragedy is that the party was making no attempt to politicise them. As a result, many of them lack the consciousness or the ability to get things done. They are not articulate or confident enough to fight for their own interests or the interests of their own community.

These women politicians, because of the focus on caste and religion, are different from the middle-class English-educated women we are so used to seeing in other political parties. They have links with the ground-level reality, they have some idea about what 80 per cent of India is all about. They are not uniformly of one class and one sentiment though – there are middle-class women like Talat and Manju Zakki as well as women like Gauri Devi and Sharda Devi who have turned their rural rootedness to advantage.

The Telugu Desam Party (Andhra Pradesh)

The rise of the Telugu Desam is closely linked with N.T. Rama Rao and his struggle to re-establish Andhra pride, in the wake of the humiliation heaped upon Andhra political leaders of all parties by the central leadership of the Congress during the eighties. Unlike the Samajwadi Party of Uttar Pradesh, this pride and identity was primarily a middle-class phenomenon in its formation, but its appeal to the masses and NTR's charisma combined to establish a large base for Telugu Desam. Its approach to women and its social agenda have also primarily been middle-class in orientation. But one must remember NTR also won many an election on the strength of his populism, on the strength of such slogans as making rice available for Rs. 2 a kilo, and prohibition.

Prohibition was a major focus in the campaign for the Lok Sabha elections of 1996 in many of the southern States. Jumping onto the bandwagon of the women's movements against arrack, the TDP attracted widespread political attention on the issue and took full electoral advantage in terms of the women's vote. The government is, as a result, committed to prohibition and to take steps to curb the liquor lobby, in spite of the heavy losses in revenues. Drinking of arrack or country liquor had emerged as a real problem among the poorer sections because valuable and limited resources are spent on drinking and the family is deprived from essential means of sustenance. Linked to this is family violence under the influence of alcohol. It led to the generation of a large women's movement. The arrack issue has forced political parties to support the cause of women. Each government in turn wanted to express its solidarity with the movement.[8]

Renuka Chowdhury, Rajya Sabha member and parliamentary leader of the TDP in Parliament, is a well-known face, having been elected to the Rajya Sabha twice. We asked Renuka Chowdhury what kind of space a regional party like TDP gave women and whether this was any different from other regional parties or the so-called national parties. Renuka Chowdhury sees herself as a strong woman who has fought for her present position in the party forcing the male leaders to recognise her potential. Her experience in the party revealed

8 Arrack was banned in Andhra Pradesh by the Congress (I) Government in December 1994—a total ban, covering all alcohol-based drinks as part of the election pledge of the Telugu Desam Party led by N.T. Rama Rao that came to power.

that hostility towards women is a part of the political system as a whole and not just of the TDP. Moreover, the space for a woman who is educated, independent, and without prior political affiliations is very small, as she would demand a share in the power and would not be satisfied with small favours bestowed by the party leadership.

Unlike most other women who come into politics she had little or no political background. "I belong to a family which was on the whole progressive, and we were all educated. There were no direct political affiliations in the family. My father belonged to the armed forces, so at one level we also had a sheltered existence. On one side, we faced the harsh reality of war but on the other side led an isolated non-political life. Growing up in a forces background however did instil in me a strong sense of nationalism. Another thing about me was that I was always a militant person. I was the college president and I was never scared of speaking my mind. Once I nearly got thrown out of college for taking up a fight with a college lecturer over a canteen issue. Everybody in my father's family was educated including his own sisters, but even then there was still a great deal of traditionalism in the functioning of the family."

Like many other Andhra men and women she was angered by the treatment meted out to Andhra Pradesh by the Central Government. She says it was in response to this feeling that, "I entered politics in 1984. This was a phase when Mrs Indira Gandhi was toppling governments and all eyes were on Andhra Pradesh. The autocratic attitude of Mrs Gandhi made me very angry and I literally went from the kitchen to the road. Till then I was just a housewife and I was also pregnant. I joined NTR and organised a strike with vast support from many local women. The surprising thing was the amount of support I received from middle-class and lower middle-class women who had till now never been outside the domains of their homes. The high-handedness of the way in which a new CM was thrust upon Andhra Pradesh had outraged their sense of democratic rights, the ordinary person took it as a affront. (The reference is to Bhaskar Rao of the Congress being sworn in as the Chief Minister.) I led the strike on the 14 August 1984 and on the 15th I was arrested. In my family this political activity had a twofold reaction – the men thought that I had political ambitions, while the women believed that my pregnancy had affected my mind adversely."

"The party or NTR (for he was the party) decided to reward me for my efforts and after 1984 I was offered the post of a Chief Officer in the Department of Women and Child. I refused, as at that time I did not want to join politics. But my refusal was interpreted as a desire for more political power and then I was given the post of Chairperson in the Department of Women and Child and under pressure from my family I accepted. My husband has been a great support in my political career."

The Telugu Desam at that point was a very dynamic party and Chowdhury reminisces: "I officially joined the Telugu Desam Party in 1985. I was attracted to the party as it consisted of young people with a new open outlook. NTR was like an unguided missile with a persona which he himself could not cope with. He was egoistic and often dictatorial but he would sometimes come up with brilliant ideas and would push for change. At this point the Congress was unattractive to me, the BJP was non-existent, the Left were too rigid about their ideas. The TDP was the most attractive; it was young, open to change, and full of activity."

Conflict with NTR was inevitable as in a culture where he was revered, she refused to treat him in the same way. "My conflict with NTR started as he realised that he could not control me. I was vulnerable as I did not have any political sugar-daddies to help me. But I stuck out and I lived in virtual political isolation in the Telugu Desam Party for 10 years. I often became a pawn for them and was sent off to campaign in a village called

Poluvandala which was ridden with factionalism and a feudal hostile system. I went in thinking I would succeed without estimating the sheer physical aggression I would face. I did fight back but this showed that the party leaders had their own way of breaking people. I was intentionally sent to such a dangerous area so that when I failed I would be accused of being a weak woman."

They tried again the next time by asking her to stand from a weak seat. "In 1986, the municipal elections were announced and I was asked to stand from Banjara Hill constituency Ward 28 which was a Congress stronghold. Everybody felt that I would lose as I had been given a weak ticket, but it so happened that although the Telugu Desam was drubbed in the elections, I won the seat. Three months later I was nominated to the Rajya Sabha as the party felt that I was too qualified for the Municipal Council. In one sense, they thought it better that I was moved out of local politics where I was becoming a hindrance."

Renuka Chowdhury was once again called upon as a star campaigner to fight the then sitting Chief Minister. "The party once again used me in 1992 when they needed somebody to stand against Vijaya Bhaskar Reddy in the Assembly by-elections. This area was a highly feudal one and girls were raped by the landlord before they even attained puberty. The CM had to resort to rigging in order to finally win the seat as I did make a dent in his campaign."

She wanted to fight the issue of rigging in court, she says. "I filed a case in the courts, but here again NTR played foul as he bribed my lawyer to withdraw from the case and I was forced to accept defeat. I would, however, like to add, that was the period when T.N. Seshan took up the task of reforming elections and making it safe for women. He was a great help. Seshan has succeeded in giving the Election Commission an identity of its own and has made the present elections safe for women to contest. He has managed to enforce a stringent code of conduct on all parties."

The conflict with NTR continued almost up to his death. She describes how, "during 1994 NTR tried to pit Laxmi Parvathi against me but it failed as I was by then a recognised face and had my own support structure. NTR was uncomfortable with my rising success and was surprised at the way in which I could articulate and attract the crowds. Finally, I just moved away and he died soon after."

The TDP under NTR was very positively inclined to women's issues. "Within the TDP the thing which was nice about NTR was that one could raise women's issues, like co-parcenary rights, that is, property rights for women. Women could talk to NTR and raise issues around women's health and education, in sharp contrast to the present Chief Minister who is hesitant on the issue of free education for the girl child. For me, the main issue for women is education. Women must be educated and be economically independent. There has to be greater gender sensitisation but this will come with education, awareness and legislation. Today the Indian woman is at the cross-roads between modernity and traditionalism."

Chowdhury is conscious of the responsibilities she bears as a woman in politics. She is categorical when she says, "From the beginning my focus was on women and I decided to work among them and motivate them. They had supported me in 1984 and would continue to do so, so I had to also protect their interest. As Chairperson I made radical changes and it was a rewarding experience. My experience in the Rajya Sabha was a great eye-opener. On one side were the lofty ideals of secularism, as in the Shah Bano case, and on the other were women asking for basic needs such as toilets. The Muslim women were not interested in Shah Bano, they did not want to discuss it, they felt that their husbands would leave them. I am completely secular in my campaigning and have a wide acceptability among both the communities. In fact, it is against my principles to campaign along communal lines."

In today's Parliament, women MPs do not come out and support other women. Many of them have strong political affiliations with leaders and do not want to displease them.

Attacking the media for their Phoolan-baiting, Chowdhury said, "I do not understand why the media is after Phoolan Devi, she did what she could to fight injustice as best as she knew. She did it for survival, she is no more or less a dacoit than others whom we do not condemn. She fought people who ill-treated her, but what about these goons who killed so many innocent people during the 1984 riots? We have a conservative morality and we have to accept change. Unlike Hindi films the rape victims here (Bhanwari Devi, Phoolan Devi) did not die. The earlier trend of women coming into politics for tokenism has to change, and in spite of differences things are bound to change. In fact, some women MPs who come into politics today are also abusing the issue of women's rights and this has become a cliché and a sham. How will you know about women's issues without being part of a movement or working at the grassroots level? In fact, if Najma Heptullah was more militant she would have taken a more firm stand during the Shah Bano controversy, and it was left to a man Arif Mohammad Khan to defend women. Tokenism is far more for the minorities and there is a great amount of pandering to the minority conservative opinion. Women also have to move away from women's issues into areas that are male domains like defence, industry, etc."

It is difficult to make common cause with other women Parliamentarians, she feels. "In today's Parliament, women MPs do not come out and support other women. Many of them have strong political affiliations with leaders and do not want to displease them. Ministers making passes is very common but most women MPs do not protest about it. Very rarely do women confront them head-on but when they do, they are like mice."

After being in Parliament for so many years she has come to recognise that each legislation must be put through the acid test of gender sensitivity. She says, "Women MPs have to work to change legislation as most legislations are not gender-friendly. We talk about the prevention of degeneration of the status of women, but nowhere is this status defined. The same is true for adoption laws and succession rights."

She points out that however talented you may be, however much experience you may have, these are not things that will determine whether you get a ministerial berth or not. She gives her own example. "I should have had the first choice for a ministerial post in the UF Government but it seems I was too strong and not liked. By my seniority I have the experience and knowledge to hold a Cabinet post. But as the normal accusation is that I am equal to 10 men and therefore cannot be considered a woman, I can fight equally. Women also face a great deal of character assassination. Men tend to assume that women are one of the perks of their high offices. Women MPs are often at fault because many of them come with the support of leaders and sugar-daddies. They do not want to raise harassment as an issue and never collectively support a woman. Moreover, if a woman complains then it would give validity to the argument that women need protection and should not join politics which is a dirty field. Jaya Prada is one example of a woman who came primarily as a glamour symbol for the TDP and because the CM was enamoured by her."

Like most independent and strong women Renuka Chowdhury did not want any special privileges for herself in the form of reservation. "In principle I am against reservation but when you have to fight with your back against the wall one has no choice. Political parties constantly complain that they cannot find enough women candidates, in truth the parties have no tickets to give to women."

Contrary to the argument against the conservatism of regional parties and its adverse effect on women's participation Renuka Chowdhury says, "I feel that the regional parties are better for women, especially in the south as they are new and have to cater to women. With 33 per cent reservation in Panchayati Raj institutions the TDP has had to consider women. After I realised the parameters of politics I realised that I enjoyed it, but it is true that the present state of politics causes disillusionment. There are no statesmen and there are no dreams, only opportunism."

Renuka Chowdhury claims that she was one of the leading lights of the anti-arrack movement in Andhra Pradesh. She says, "I led the anti-arrack movement. I was approached by the women to organise their movement which I did and all the political parties supported me in this except the Congress. All the subsequent movements are a fall-out of that. I did a survey of the areas and realised that development was the least in the liquor-dominated regions." But today, she feels, the lack of any social reform movement along with the ban is damaging the cause. "Spurious liquor haunts and illegal smuggling have also started. We have to realise that the alcoholic while being an offender is also a victim and needs to be treated medically. The ban has led to 2.5 lakh families being unemployed and one has to provide financial help to them first. The banning of liquor in 5 star hotels does not make sense."

The regional parties, more so than ever before, have definitely given a new impetus to the inclusion of women in the political stream, mostly because of the relative newness of these parties themselves. Women find entry into these parties

The regional parties, more so than ever before, have definitely given a new impetus to the inclusion of women in the political stream, mostly because of the relative newness of these parties themselves.

easier as they do not have to struggle against party history and old established traditions. This trend also offers hope of a new type of woman coming to Parliament and Assemblies whose concerns have common cause with the vast majority of women in this country rather than representing only a section. The elite middle-class women across parties have been limited by their own class perceptions, whereas women recruited on the basis of caste considerations appear as yet to lack the progressive political perspective that is vital for a vibrant and responsive polity. However, women in politics are fast changing even if their parties are not.

No Room at the Top 9

The problem of women in politics can be located at different levels—history, tradition, patriarchal political structures, and the way democracy works in this country. Historically, the national movement was marked by a selective adoption of liberal slogans, with no or very little questioning of the bases of many social evils like caste, patriarchy or even the widespread acceptance of the sanctity of the *shastras*. So the change we thought had taken place was more symbolic than substantive. If we look back in terms of important women-related issues, many of our most revered leaders of the national movement do not appear in a very good light. One wonders how the question of raising the age of marriage from 10 to 12 could have elicited such a hostile and negative response from our leaders (especially in the context in which it was raised[1]) and how it could have posed a threat to Indian culture and tradition. The introduction of the Hindu Code Bill had elicited a similar response, while the greatest hostility was expressed in the context of the issues of bigamy and property rights for daughters. In more recent times, a Bill to grant co-parcenary rights in ancestral property to women in Andhra Pradesh was met with a similar hostile reaction. The responses to the Muslim Woman's Bill and *Sati* are also part of the same legacy.

[1] The Age of Consent Bill brought to the Legislature in 1891 sought to raise the legal age of marriage from 10 to 12. Conservative elements within the Congress condemned the Bill and accused those who had introduced it as "enemies of Hindu civilisation". The immediate cause for raising this matter in the Legislative Council was the death of an 11-year-old girl Phulmani caused due to forced sexual intercourse (rape) by her husband.

Historical and Ideological Bias

While women could be expected to set aside conventional sex roles for nationalist goals, there was no debate on a permanent restructuring of traditional sex roles and making it an acceptable pattern of women's life-style. It was generally accepted that this was permissible only at times of crisis, and that otherwise the woman's primary responsibility was exclusively to the home. That is why there was a considerable decline in the number of women participating within the Congress after freedom—the time of crisis was now over and women could go back to their kitchens. Politics remained a male prerogative thereafter. Since this ideology was never questioned, socially conservative elements were never identified and marked out. As a result they have since remained powerful and articulate within the Congress on issues relating to women. The overall liberal political position of the Congress and the fact that it spearheaded the national movement often makes us forget and at times overlook these facts.

The Congress Party that took over governance after freedom retained much of the conservative character of the pre-independence Congress. In later years Mrs Gandhi being a woman did not in any way change the situation, in fact it created a facade of the Congress being pro-women which was contrary to the day-to-day reality of its politics. It misled many conscious women into believing in her. The men were already hostile, and Mrs Gandhi saw to it that no other woman in the party acquired power. The only period in the Congress when a relatively liberal atmosphere prevailed was during Rajiv Gandhi's tenure, but ultimately he too had to compromise with conservative sections, on the issue of the Muslim Women's Bill, for instance. Ambiguity, ambivalence and opportunism have thus been the hall-mark of the Congress on issues related to women

This conservative "cultural nationalistic" perspective has dominated most other political parties as well, and no conscious attempt has been made by any of them to abandon it. The BJP, on the contrary, has further refined it in the current context. Women are seen as the repositories of culture and, therefore, must be guarded and protected against change, especially change brought about by Westernisation. This image has to now accommodate the compulsions of modern living such as education, work and a host of other activities that compel women to move out of the house. But the party continues to see the primary role of women as mothers and wives, as home-makers and bearers of children, preferably sons. All rights are subservient to this primary role, which is defined in terms of prescribed rituals and unquestioning subordination to the family as taught in the RSS *shakhas*. Submission to patriarchal authority is promoted by the BJP Mahila Samiti, which expects women to maintain the peace in the family. Career choices and even organisational work in the party are subject to family sanction. It is only when this key institution and its structure is protected that the nation is safe from its 'enemies'.

The CPI(M) has an equally well-defined ideological position on women that is the most liberal and progressive in outlook amongst all the political parties. It clearly sees the position of women in class society as exploitative and identifies institutional structures that are the source of their oppression. The situation of women is not seen as a social evil but as a systemic and structural component of the social and economic relations of society. However, the colonial experience and the struggle with imperialism, and the remnants of the cultural nationalism of the freedom struggle, have all prevented the party from carrying its stated position to its logical conclusion. The constant struggle with the "other" (the colonial masters or the imperialists) prevented the party from introspection about its own cultural underpinnings on issues of gender. So, the culture of defence against the so-called enemy became a defence of many of the retrograde values that kept women in this subservient position. Dominant middle-class values that should have been subjected to rigorous questioning became the accepted national ideology. This dominance of middle-class consciousness and values is still evident in many positions the party takes from time to time. Hence the contradiction persists between progressive affirmative action on wider issues of gender justice and a lack of analysis of gender biases implicit in middle-class notions of culture, social and familial relationships. Women within the party have changed because of their own experience and struggle, but since the debate was never conducted on issues closer to home (the family and the party) the men have not felt it necessary to change their patriarchal attitudes towards women.

On the whole, because of the overall ideological commitment of the party towards equality, the party and its members have found it difficult to strike conservative public postures. Therefore, the CPI(M) and its frontal organisations have consistently taken progressive positions and played an active role in support of women's issues, unlike other political parties. Also, unlike in the regional parties, caste and religion do not play a part in democratic left politics, and this has freed women from the caste and religious oppression that is characteristic of parties like the BJP or the Samajwadi Party.

The situation was different in States where regional parties emerged in response to the post-independence context, anti-Brahmin movements, language agitation and reassertion of regional pride and identity. The political history of such parties as the Samajwadi Party in Uttar Pradesh is much shorter, and their priorities and compulsions are very different. For the Samajwadi Party, we found caste and religion to be the dominant factors in political calculations and decision-making. This conservatism is a natural result of the conditions in which such parties have been formed: First, these parties were formed due to local compulsions rather than nationalist perceptions, and to that extent there was no formulated policy towards women on any kind of ideological basis. Their response to the question of women's political participation, as to other issues, was primarily based on caste considerations and specific vote-banks, and was more in the nature of an ad hoc response depending on the specific situation. Many women who joined the SP actually believed in Mulayam Singh's personal commitment to the women's cause and that became the ideological reference point for the party's commitment to women.

Organisational and Class Bias

There has been no remarkable change in the caste or class character of women within the Congress—women in the Mahila Congress have little grassroots-level experience or commitment. Neither has the Congress made any effort to train and bring in women from other sections of society. BJP is also a party rooted in the middle class and has always been marked by middle class conservatism. Women are therefore not encouraged or expected to do much grassroots level work which takes them outside the house. The women's political activity is supposed to work through family networking. This has been one of the main reasons why the woman's wing of the party has not grown at the same pace, as say the left women's organisations. In order to overcome this middle class bias the party is now making special efforts to mobilise lower caste women.

The CPI(M) leadership as well as that of its mass organisations is also primarily from the middle class, nevertheless, even the middle-class party women within the mass organisations (like the AIDWA) maintain certain grassroots-level linkages with other women, they have a greater awareness of social reality and are not as cut off from other sections of society as their counterparts in other parties. The party also consciously attempts to make the working class, peasantry and other 'toiling masses' as it calls them, its major constituency hence mobilisation of women from these classes has been an ideal which the party is committed to, even if it has not been able to actually achieve it.

Participation at the grassroots level becomes important because the need for change and the urgency for change is felt by these women the most in their struggle for day-to-day existence, whereas the elite women, who have so far controlled political power, are not subject to the same kind of compulsions for change. It is only with the emergence of the regional parties specially those committed to the backward communities and relying on their vote banks (Samajwadi Party, Janata Dal) that we find women from a different class emerging . As a result a great turmoil is taking place in relation to norms and expected patterns of behaviour. Ridicule is heaped on those who appear unacquainted with the rules of the game, like Phoolan Devi, both by men and women of different political parties.

Party Structure: Where are the Women?

The visibility of women within the organisational structure of the Congress party is low, both at the national and local levels. Not a single General Secretary of the Congress Party is a woman. When adequate numbers of women are not present in the State Congress Committee the quota is filled through nomination, but these nominated members do not have the right to vote. Women's issues thus hardly ever get discussed, because there are always more important issues on the agenda.

The Congress party works through centres of power located in particular leaders, almost all male. It is often the case that women who acquire power in the party are those who are either close to the central big-wigs or the PCC chiefs at the state level. Action of party bosses are rarely questioned. What is surprising is that this mode of functioning, problematic as it may seem, is the way Congress has always functioned. Today, when people want more democratic space within society and within parties the Congress is unable to accommodate these aspirations. The hostility of men towards women in the party has been consistent and pronounced, but today this hostility has almost turned into a conflict, where many women feel that men would not even hesitate, at times, to harm women. These fears exist more at the state level. The Congress does not allow sharing of power and women are not strong enough to fight for their rights. Women feel that the party does not ever speak up for women, and when it does, it is mere tokenism. The conservative men in the party, because of increasing pressure from the women's movement are, however, becoming more wary of articulating their views in public.

Leaders of the Mahila Congress may be encouraged to make speeches on ceremonial occasions, but their programmes of action are not taken seriously. Many Congress members feel that more women would be willing to come to the Congress, if only the Mahila Congress exhibited some direction and activity. The Mahila Congress on the one hand has not been able to radicalise itself, and on the other it can no longer provide even middle-class women avenues to give expression to their political aspirations, especially at the State level, and this may drive many of them to the BJP. The State leadership does not have the initiative, the creativity, or the organisational infrastructure to deal with the rising aspirations of women in politics. The party is fragmented, it has no agenda, no target, no work, and infighting makes functioning even more difficult. In States where the women's movement is weak, the women's wing of the party is in a worse situation. In these States there is hardly any awareness of women's rights. To talk of mobilisation in the form of a women's movement is very far indeed.

The BJP party hierarchy is also characterised by the absence of women at decision-making levels and the presence of figures like the Rajmata Scindia, as she herself put it, is more decorative than influential. Sushma Swaraj is an exception rather than the rule. Despite a certain defensiveness and hesitancy on the part of BJP women to criticise the party in any way, most of them acknowledged the unwillingness of men to share power. They admitted that the question of equality caused friction within the party, as men were not ready to accept women in positions of authority. Women and women's organisations are not given much importance in the BJP. There is little stress on formal organisational status or training. The women's organisation is entirely nominated, there is thus no vibrancy or strength that is characteristic of a democratic organisation. Mobilisation is primarily through extension of the family influence through kinship and through neighbourhood association. The need for other means of mobilisation is not felt. Being a cadre based party, it has never lacked direction or discipline. However, its scope and functioning is limited by those very ideological compulsions which give it its sense of purpose.

The BJP has recognised the need to cater to the increasing number of educated middle-class women who form an important segment of their constituency. The party is trying to relate its own approach to the change in the life-styles of women from the days of their mothers and grandmothers. So there is consciousness of the need to create a new image which is a combination of tradition and modernity—a process of political accommodation recognising the need for new platforms and new issues. The BJP has shown a certain amount of versatility and flexibility in appropriating and moulding modernity to serve its essentially conservative ideology. It wants to permanently carve out a constituency among upper-class and upper-caste women by meeting their dual need of social and political status and of conformity and acceptability. Therefore, it has championed the cause of reservation for women. It hopes to emerge as the champion of the women's cause, even while others are divided on the issue.

However, today there is an increasing recognition that this way of functioning has limited the base of the BJP's women's wing to upper-caste and upper-class women, and that there is a need to mobilise Dalit and Other Backward Castes women. The BJP, is now getting its act together after the 33 per cent reservation in Panchayati Raj institutions has come about. How far this is a response to necessity and how much of it will be converted into conviction for a new political role for women is yet to be seen.

The under-representation of women in leadership positions within the party is quite evident in the CPI(M) also. There has been criticism of the CPI(M) for its inability to mobilise more women at the grassroots level, enabling them to rise in the party hierarchy. Pressure from Communist women has forced the party to accept increasing involvement of women in the decision-making process and today they have the opportunity to raise their problems more frequently and more assertively in different party forums. Unfortunately, efforts for adequate representation of women have not necessarily found reflection in the party organisation itself. At the same time rise of some women in the party has not necessarily led to an overall increase in women's influence, and whenever women have tried to force an issue that goes against conventionally held notions, they face tremendous opposition. The CPI(M) women felt that the party could afford to be more attentive and considerate to correct the imbalance in women's representation at all levels of the organisation.

The 33 per cent reservation for women in Panchayati Raj institutions has brought into focus the fact that there is a need to bring more and more rural women into the party. But the problem is that these women are often not equipped to become members of the CPI(M), as the party expects a certain level of consciousness for membership—not everybody can become a CPI(M) member. This becomes a great handicap in the case of women. Also, women have difficulty in attending party schools and study circles because of their timing (when they are held late at night) and the pressure of housework. The party has not yet developed any programme to meet the special requirements of rural women, despite the fact that most of the women activists felt that if such an effort was made, they could easily be mobilised.

Another criticism of the functioning of AIDWA, has been that its politics frequently extended beyond the limited sphere of women's issues which has resulted in allegations of its tailing the CPI(M). It is difficult to assess the relative autonomy of organisations like the AIDWA in setting their own agenda, but what is certainly visible is an attempt by the women to present to the party their own set of demands. The lack of public access to inner party debates on such issues makes it difficult to come to any definite conclusions. But one thing is evident: the organisation has grown substantially over the years in terms of its membership. In places like Rajasthan, the AIDWA has been able to establish a presence for itself, despite the low visibility of the CPI(M) itself. It has established a certain credibility for itself within the wider women's movement, and at times has even contributed towards politicising important women's issues.

The Samajwadi Party remains very much a one-man show and there is hardly any visible division of power within the organisation specially at election time. There was also no sign of any effective functioning organisational structure that was in control of party affairs. The structuring of the party around leaders rather than ideology makes it very difficult for women to get access to sources of power except by hanging around political leaders. The women's wing of the Samajwadi Party has little significance within the decision-making structure of the party. Primarily established as a show-piece to show the party's concern and active role in support of women, the membership is marked by a set of opportunistic middle-class women who are based mainly in Lucknow and who hardly do any grassroots-level work. Other women in the organisation are there due to caste considerations and very few joined on their own.

Areas of Discrimination

At one level, the **party's ideology** itself may be discriminatory (BJP) on the other hand its ambiguity in a traditional society may leave adequate space for discrimination (Congress). But what of a party that clearly spells out a progressive ideology (CPI(M)? Talking about discrimination, women of the CPI(M) felt that there was no universal attitude of men towards women within the party, each individual brings to the party his or her own tradition and culture. Party workers at times exhibit a sense of lack of gender equality because they carry with them their traditional value systems which are often feudal and patriarchal, into the party. Much of the discrimination against women in the party is because of the attitudes of these individuals. But at the same time women assert that the party does not try to change the attitude of both men and women who come to the party or make them more gender sensitive.

The **nature of electoral politics** in this country effectively marginalises women and women's issues from the political agenda. Congress women feel that electoral politics, at times, limits the kind of support women politicians would like to extend to members of their own sex, since they realise that they cannot win elections on women's issues alone. This is perhaps due to the fact that the women who have come into politics are few in number, and represent a very narrow section of society. Most of them are still hesitant to identify themselves with women's issues, claiming that women form only one section of their constituency and till recently not the determining section. Also, elections are largely conducted by men and with men's support. One noticed that even during the campaigns of women candidates in the 1996 elections the entourage largely consisted of men, and that the agenda was predominantly a male one. Electoral expediency requires women participants to compromise to survive in the man's world of politics.

The CPI(M) women found it **difficult ideologically to**

prioritise women's issues over other issues especially economic issues, although the AIDWA has perhaps been the only political women's organisation which has mobilised women on issues which have at times been in direct conflict with tradition (Muslim Women's Bill and the Anti-Sati Act). The BJP **prioritised religion and tradition** above all other issues thus effectively marginalising women and regional parties work under compulsions of caste, religion or other local pressures, the issues of women were not high on their political agenda. The greatest compulsions for avoiding women's issues, however, is of keeping vote-banks intact. This has made most parties shy away from any issue which directly confronts the traditional beliefs of any community, thus inadvertently playing into the hands of conservative elements.

Discrimination against women within political parties, both its basis and motive force, remained the same. **Men were not willing to lose seats to women**. It may be for this reason women from all three political parties identified ticket allotment stage of elections as the greatest point of discrimination against women in politics. Grassroots-level workers are often ignored, even though they do all the work. The State leaderships are particularly conservative in their approach as far as the distribution of tickets to women is concerned. Men do not want women in politics in the first place, so they do not put up a woman candidate for a winning seat. When political parties do think of fielding women candidates, they are generally given losing seats and the example of their defeat is used to deprive other women of party tickets. Pramila Dandavate elaborates, "First, they do not have faith that women can get elected. Second, they feel even when a woman does manage to get elected, she will not be in a position to open her mouth and do anything fruitful in Parliament. Third, men feel that politics is a man's world. They would just like to have a woman along with them like a flower-pot in a drawing room or *achar* in the meal. But they do not like to see them in responsible positions, on an equal footing."

The situation in parties like the Samajwadi Party was similar. Hostility of party leaders in giving tickets to women was marked, and all the common features and means of discrimination used by leaders of other parties were visible here as well. The form of discrimination at the regional level was cruder and more apparent and since most of the women here are perhaps intellectually less equipped to deal with the situation, they are more disadvantaged and vulnerable. Importantly, there was no ideological reference point that could be used to compel leaders to take a more just or humane approach to the question of women's representation and matters were made worse by the lack of any party organisational structure and planning

The Political Environment

According to women from all parties the political environment was not conducive to women's participation in politics. Congress and the BJP women claimed that it is always assumed women cannot succeed on their own; they have to piggyback on the favours of some leading politician or the other, while men succeed merely because of their capability. As a result, successful women often have to face character assassination, irrespective of how old they are.

We have clearly seen that most women who have come into politics have done so with the active support of their families and if the families are powerful enough women are able to sustain their position in the political arena. Family backing protects women from harassment from male colleagues. Because of their family status, men are forced to tolerate certain women and accommodate their views, which implies that without these advantages, women would not be taken seriously. The CPI(M) women also felt that family support enabled women to enter politics. The family can free women from domestic responsibility and help them in their political work when required. If members of the family are politically influential it makes the process of getting tickets and fighting elections much easier.

Most parties, except the Communists, expect women candidates to raise their own resources by means "fair or foul", and this becomes extremely difficult for women who do not, cannot, or will not, have the required connections with the underworld or black money. The net result is, women who lack the money and resources to sustain their electoral campaign cannot think of venturing into politics. Since women are not able to mobilise funds from all kinds of criminal sources, they require the support of the party both for resources and manpower, both of which are essential for winning an election, and both are rarely forthcoming. In the absence of such support mechanisms, women participants and political aspirants at all levels feel isolated, weak, frustrated and, in the end, apathetic. And the fact of the matter is that the political parties are yet to come forward to provide that kind of support. The Congress women claimed that **lack of party support and poor organisational structure**, especially at the local level, further weakens the woman's position to bargain for positions within the party or to demand tickets.

National Postures and State Politics

The attitude of Congress and BJP politicians in Madhya Pradesh and Rajasthan **in the day-to-day functioning in different political forums** also revealed conscious discrimination if not hostility. They described how frivolously their issues were treated by men in the Assembly. Women hardly got an opportunity to speak in the Assembly and when they did, they were heckled. One legislator from Rajasthan went so far as to say that in the Assembly the situation of women is very similar to that in the police station and courts. There is very little change in the attitude of the male leadership towards women and there is very little support within the party to change the situation.

The situation in West Bengal was relatively different and yet similar. Within the ideology of the CPI(M), there should be no differences at the regional and national levels in the party's position on women-related issues. However, local pressures and lack of exposure make party women at the local level more hesitant and local party men more rigid. **Discrimination is evident in the State Committees where women are not involved in decision-making**. Woman after woman stressed that it was important for women to fight and be heard and to pressurise the party into accepting the woman's point of view. The middle-class party women find it easier to do this, but the poor rural women are still not equipped to undertake such struggles.

Need for Opportunities

The Congress women pointed out that legal reform is not enough; it is necessary for political parties to give women opportunities to exercise their rights. Since they have not done so in the past fifty years, on what basis are they to assume that the situation will change today or tomorrow? It is in this context that the issue of reservation has been raised. The Congress women, from their own experience, also recognised that men will be hostile to this demand whatever their public utterances.

The BJP women have come to recognise that without reservation they can never hope to get adequate representation either in the party, or through the party, in positions of power. The party, on the other hand, wants to consolidate its base among middle class women through its support of 33 per cent reservation and therefore it was quick to silence the doubts raised by Uma Bharati. Most Communist women, do have doubts whether reservation would guarantee effective sharing of power and do not favour reservation *per se* but felt that, given the hold of tradition and conservative attitudes, women are left with no alternative but to demand reservation.

Individually, women of the Samajwadi Party came out strongly in favour of the 33 per cent reservation for women in Assemblies and Parliament. However, this was before the issue of OBC reservation was introduced into the argument. The support may not be so categorical any longer now that divisions have been created on the basis of caste. One thing is quite certain, for most of the Samajwadi women the prime identity is that of caste and not of gender. In this dispute they may conveniently forget the fact that when Dalit women are oppressed or raped it is not the Dalit men who come out in protest but women of all castes and classes who have experienced and understand gender oppression.

Ideology and consciousness is central to political perspective, as it provides the basis of the emancipatory space that a party has for all the sections of society that it represents. This is clearly visible in the way Communist women have struggled against those who have sought to hold them back. At the same time even they could not deny discrimination which works on a different plane altogether, all women in the political process had experienced and recognised this discrimination and had felt an increasing sense of frustration at the unwillingness of the present party structures to accept the lacuna of under-representation and correct it. The cards of tradition, religion and caste are all stacked in favour of men; at the same time, lack of legitimacy, the burden of alternative prescribed commitments and the lack of advantage of wealth are on the side of women. In the light of the experiences of these women, it becomes evident that reservation is crucial for their effective participation in politics. The question is not of power alone but also of the need to legitimise women's presence in the public sphere. That is why visibility becomes so important. Women in significant numbers would make a difference—they would speak out, and what is more important, be heard on issues related to their sex. They may be able to change laws in favour of women, present a legitimate female perspective.

Women in India today are agitating at the doors of Parliament, demanding reservation for 33 per cent of the seats. The issue at stake here is more complex than it may seem. It is not only a question of a few more or a few less women in the corridors of Parliament and legislatures but also a response to the fact that a large section of society has historically been denied its legitimate share in the exercise of political power, power that ultimately determines its destiny. In this demand for reservation, women are also raising their voice against a system which has consistently denied them space by harnessing the forces of tradition in order to marginalise and trivialise their role. After all, what is democracy if 50 per cent of the population have little or no say in it? To ignore such demands is to fail to understand and come to terms with the forces of history. History will judge this epoch in terms of its response to the demands of women for their legitimate share in democratic power, as it did earlier epochs on the basis of access to power of other marginalised sections of our social and political system. This will unleash a corresponding tension to rectify imbalances as did earlier struggles within our social system. Reservation of seats for women in Panchayats has shown that it has tremendous implications, not merely in terms of the number of women entering the public arena and holding public office, but also in terms of the social, economic and political impact that these reservations have had for the total system.

It is for these reasons that women are increasingly demanding political roles for themselves. They recognise that constitutional guarantees do not ensure effective participation and that these cannot ensure political equality. Hence the need to gain entry into political institutions and in the functioning of the state, and to share control over the power the state exercises. This alone would lead to a situation where women are able to reverse the existing situation which has consistently been against their interests, and bring about the necessary changes in policy and the social structure so as to ensure a more equitable and humane order.

The role of women's participation in elected bodies should not be undervalued. Elections are after all a forum for self-government and democracy, they are significant in drawing the attention of the nation to the problems and needs of disadvantaged sections; the manifestos, campaigns, promises made by individual candidates, track record and future course of action of political parties are indicative of national concerns as well as mandates for action. Proper selection of candidates in an election is vital if this representative democracy is to function in the interests of a majority of the population that is depressed and disadvantaged. Hence, opportunities for participation at this level are significant for the adoption of policies and measures for women's development. As Sushila Kaushik has rightly pointed out, "Democracy does not and cannot operate by proxy."[2] Women, who form a major section of society, have increasingly come to feel that their interests have not been adequately represented thus far, and they have rightly deduced that this may be because they have not worked effectively within the political system and political parties as a pressure group demanding representation in adequate numbers. We have seen that all the political parties (Congress, BJP and CPI (M)) albeit to different extents, are perpetrators of this neglect, we can no longer imagine that they will voluntarily give women the space so long denied to them.

Strong and dynamic women who would not dream of appropriating privilege, are today talking of reservation because they have come to recognise that the "political Brahmins" (male politicians) will not give "temple entry" (in

2 Kaushik, *Why Women in Legislatures*, Presented at the Meet of Parliamentarians, 19 November 1996, organised by National Commission for Women .

the corridors of power) without reservation. This hierarchy is so rigid that the natural processes of democracy and constitutional guarantees have not been able to make a dent in these fortresses of power. The analogy with caste here is intentional because the system practises the same kind of insularity *vis-à-vis* women as it has traditionally done in terms of caste restrictions. A woman Assembly candidate from Uttar Pradesh articulated this frustration effectively when she said, with all the vehemence that comes from understanding the force of the feudal power that still exists in rural areas: "These men will never give us power. We will have to put our hands into their throats and pull it out from their stomachs, that is the only way."[3] Therefore, women like Pramila Dandavate who were earlier not in favour of reservation at the Assembly and Parliamentary level are convinced now that unless the demand of reservation for women (33 per cent) is met, there is no possibility in the near future of women coming into politics in large numbers.

The demand for reservation should not therefore be seen as either a gift or a privilege that women are seeking. For most women it is the last straw and a desperate measure to ensure their coming into the political mainstream. Their participation becomes vital in the context of the adoption of development strategies that are negative and harmful to women. Combined with this is the socio-political context where atrocities against women are on the rise—be it communal or caste riots, peasants' or workers' struggles, cases of dowry deaths or sexual assaults, women are increasingly becoming direct victims. The continuance of feudal patriarchal dominance along with the rise of fundamentalism and Rightist extremism poses a great threat to the hard-won gains of the last few decades. In this context, political rights come to mean the ability of women to prevent a situation where they are so used and abused that it is

3 The original in Hindi is as follows: *Yeh mard hamen satta kabhi nahin denge, inke gale may haath dalkar pet se nikalna padega.*

synonymous with the right to their very existence.

Men have been hostile to the idea of an increasing number of women coming into politics and of sharing power with women and it was well known that despite the electoral commitment of all parties on the issue of 33 per cent reservation for women in Assemblies and Parliament, this Bill would not be adopted easily. Yet, the subversive and virulent opposition to the Reservation Bill has come as a thunderbolt.

It is interesting to see in what kind of political environment women are making this demand. On the one hand, we have all parties across the board supporting the issue with firm commitments in their election manifestos, and on the other, each party is trying to undermine the efforts of other parties to get the Bill through in order to take individual credit. The debate on reservation in the press shows how different sections have responded to the issue. As Mrinal Pande points out,[4] one can clearly see the hostility of some sections through the responses of the media and certain politicians. Despite the lip-service paid to the issue of women's participation the attitudes of most people in the game have not changed and there is a clear contradiction between what they profess and what they actually believe and have been practising. Pande shows how the media either ignores or is openly hostile to women's attempts to focus on the demand for reservation. She quotes *The Patriot* of 11 June 1996:

> Although it is known that some sections of people in the country, including the women, should take more active interest in public life, this cannot be ensured by a system of reverse preference to ensure quota for women in the legislature. This is the surest way of ensuring that women do not achieve equal status in life.

The message is absolutely clear: women have already been given equality by the Constitution (on paper at least), so what

[4] *The Hindustan Times*, Magazine Section, 21 July 1996.

is all this fuss about? And even if it were not guaranteed by the Constitution, such support to women is going to lead them to more misery and dependency. Women, according to this theory, says Pande, are unequal because they are dependent. But the theorists also add that if this situation is reversed by law, women would still remain unequal, almost as if it were due to 'God-given *karma*'. She cites this as but one example of our national double-speak on issues relating to empowerment of women. The media, be it the Shah Bano case or the Bhanwari Devi case, has consistently endorsed the traditional Indian view that politics is a male arena and women's issues, if they are ever to be raised, will ultimately have to be viewed against 'national' (as Pande says, read male) interests and priorities. And why should women bother running around parties asking for tickets anyway, in what is a 'corrupt den of thieves'?

As Pramila Ḍandavate[5] says, "I have been fighting for the cause for women's political participation for decades now. It is a well known fact that men do not want to share power with women. The criterion in giving a ticket is always: will she win, does she have funds, will she assert herself? Do all men who fight elections win? And how many of them make it on their own without a godfather? When the 73rd Amendment gave reservation for women at the local level, there were over ten lakh women who were elected as Panchayat members all over the country. Why can't that formula be replicated at the national

[5] Senior Parliamentarian and woman activist. She has time and again raised the issue of women's rights in the House and on the streets. In 1980-84, it was thanks to her that a number of private member Bills for enhancing the status of women were introduced including those dealing with dowry prohibition and registration of marriage. She also moved a resolution for setting up a National Commission for Women with statutory powers. She was the first President of the Mahila Dakshita Samiti, the women's wing of the Janata Dal. She is also currently the General Secretary of the party. Despite being an activist and a person who is aware of discrimination against women, she was made to prioritise her husband's political career and ambitions over her own. Throughout her life she has struggled with her own aspirations and capabilities on the one side and her prescribed role defined both by party and tradition on the other.

level too? I support reservation as in the present situation there is no choice. But this has to be looked at not as the solution but as a step forward. Once women come out in the open they should be able to fight equally." Dandavate is clear that 33 per cent reservation for women does not mean that the rest are reserved for men. It should be made clear that 33 per cent is the minimum that should be given to women and it should in no way set a limit. She feels it is essential in order to implement development policies and to cope with problems like the feminisation of poverty. With 33 per cent reservation politicians will have to take women's perspectives into consideration, but along with this there should be an attempt at political education, training programmes, and orientation workshops so that women can fulfil their political responsibilities in a better fashion.

Mohini Giri, Chairperson of the National Commission for Women, feels reservation is the only way that women will be able to get tickets to contest elections. In the 1996 general elections many articulate and politically strong women like Margaret Alva, Mrinal Gore, Pramila Dandavate and Renuka Choudhury did not get tickets. Many women were pushed into reserved constituencies (e.g., Meira Kumar, Kumari Selja), while others were merely proxies for men (e.g., Mrs Kamal Nath and Chhabeli Netam). There is always talk of the dummies and ineffective women who sit in Parliament but no one mentions what Sushma Swaraj calls the several Mauni Babas that sit in every Parliament. Most women politicians seem to think alike on the issue but some like Girija Vyas do think that the reverse preference should be thought of only within a fixed time-frame. Others feel a surge of optimism: "More women means more schools, primary health care, upgradation of skills." This impact, they say, is already being felt in the case of the Panchayati Raj. But women must consciously represent the interest of the vast mass of women.

Senior men politicians such as V.P. Singh are sceptical whether the patriarchal structure will give way to women so easily. Fifty years of a futile wait for the male-centric political system to deliver women from the daily grind of their lives, has shown women that it is time they moved in and seized the initiative like the Dalits, OBCs and minorities have done. Otherwise all major decisions on issues ranging from development priorities to family welfare packages would leave them out again.

Mrinal Pande rightly points out: "The last half a century, it now seems, was a painful period, during which our educated urban women were reinventing the wheel before relearning the lessons the Dalits could have taught them: that despite India's becoming a democracy, a feudal and false mythology of inferiority grounded in gender and caste was used time and again to keep women away from the political mainstream. Together, both the women and the Dalits have been victims of the grossly underpaid or unpaid labour system on which the Indian nation and society have rested for centuries. The Dalits were the first to realise and question this. The backwards were next, and now women are asking the same question. Revolts against birth-based systems of discrimination can be both contagious and national. So the latest demand for the 33 per cent reservation for women in Parliament and State Assemblies is a natural organic development of the events of the last 50 years."

Gender bias in political circles has not disappeared due to the necessity of mouthing politically correct statements on women's political participation.

"But ever since the ruling coalition announced their intention to introduce reservation for women as promised under their Common Minimum Programme, a form of collective encephalitis seems to have broken out in our male-centric political parties. Symptoms include an almost incoherent rush of feminist terminology such as gender-based imbalance, gender-sensitisation of members, helping the disadvantaged females in the 'poverty stricken sector' and than a total inability to explain logically exactly why in their personal opinion there should be reservation for women. Having purged themselves of a little speech, about women's empowerment, the party spokespersons usually lapse into oblivion, with no regard for how exactly their party is going to relate to this proposed Bill and why. As the Parliament session where this is to be debated, draws close, the illness grows more severe."

In a panel discussion held at the Women's Press Club in 1996 V.P. Singh warned of a backlash which women will now have to face.

> Since the idea is a politically correct one, parties will not rush to oppose it in public or in print. But they will try their best to scuttle it by first raising legal bogies and then referring the matter to one Select Committee or the other.[6]

He proved to be almost prophetic.

The faults and limitations of Panchayati Raj reservation are constantly thrown in women's faces as a good reason for not moving ahead with the reservation in Assemblies and Parliament. But as Margaret Alva[7] says,

> We are seeing before our eyes, the rise of a whole new cadre of politically aware women, who are empowering themselves as they move along the mainstream. So what if they are a little raw and not too confident. Given the time and experience they will learn just as the Indian men learnt a bare 50 years ago.[8]

Attempts to divide women have already started, as Pande observes: "Male Right-wing leaders and their media counterparts have often used divide and conquer to obfuscate

[6] Quoted in Pande, ibid.

[7] Minister for Women and Child Development in the previous Congress Government.

[8] Quoted in Pande, ibid.

reform measures, by separating along caste-conscious lines, and in many ways they have succeeded."

Syed Shahabuddin has opposed women's reservation in Parliament because it would enable the "upper-castes to push their women in thereby gaining on the swings what they lose on the roundabouts" (because of the Mandal reservations).

Geeta Mukherjee has been articulate in her support for the 33 per cent Reservation Bill. She and other women parliamentarians across party lines, proclaimed that they are going to see to it that the Bill is not only tabled but passed this winter session (1996). She says, "As far as the 33 per cent Bill is concerned, the Government will have to place the Bill in Parliament during the winter session. Initially the Bill was only to be introduced in the previous session. But once the women members of the Rajya Sabha (the Upper House of Parliament) decided to get it passed we also joined in. The problem was raised by Uma Bharati on the question of Scheduled Caste, Scheduled Tribe and OBC reservation.

The recent developments on the Reservation Bill make it evident that there is opposition to the Bill from men in general, with one section trying to legitimise this by raising the issue of OBC reservation. In spite of the earlier assurance by Prime Minister, Deve Gowda, that on the basis of the Select Committee Report the Bill would be tabled and passed in the winter session (1996) of the Parliament, he has expressed his failure to do so and the fate of the Bill remains uncertain.[9]

Women have changed or are changing, but men are yet to change. Perhaps it is irrational to expect that a group that has enjoyed power legitimately for hundreds of years will suddenly recognise the unfairness of it all and willingly surrender their power in the cause of justice and fairplay. Perhaps when

[9] The BJP and the CPI(M) are supporting the passage of the Bill, the Congress is ambivalent, while Janata Dal and the Samajwadi Party of the United Front are opposing the Bill till a quota within 33 per cent is reserved for OBC and minority communities.

women asked for 33 per cent reservation they overlooked the fact that this is how it would be perceived. Who willingly surrenders power? No ruling class in history has done so. Power has to be wrested and women have to struggle for their rights. Men certainly are not going to give it to them willingly.